THE BIO THAT GOES FOR *BLOKE* ON

- Ewan's rock 'n' roll past
- The U.S. state he loves to hate
- His sexiest and weirdest roles
- The actor who inspired him since age six —and connects him to *Star Wars*
- Real musical skills he used in *Brassed Off*
- The dramatic *ER* guest shot
- CDs he can't live without
- The motorcycle dream
- Hollywood bashing—McGregor style
- And much, much more!

Ewan McGregor

Ewan McGregor

CHRIS NICKSON

St. Martin's Paperbacks

EWAN McGREGOR

Copyright © 1999 by Chris Nickson.

Cover photograph by © Lorenzo Agius/Outline.

ISBN: 0-312-96910-4

Printed in the United States of America

St. Martin's Paperbacks edition / April 1999

10 9 8 7 6 5 4 3 2 1

FOR GRAHAM, AGAIN AND ALWAYS

Acknowledgments

I'm always happy to thank my wonderful agent, Madeleine Morel, who does such an excellent job on my behalf. Working with John Rounds on this project was, as it always is, a huge pleasure, and I appreciate the opportunity to write about an actor I admire. Stephanie Ogle, at Cinema Books in Seattle, remains a constant treasure and a wonderful source of material for me. The British Film Institute should not be forgotten. As with any book, there is a cast of thousands—well, several dozen, anyway—who contribute their two-cents' worth, their friendship, and their support. My parents, Ray and Betty Nickson, who have always been there for me, Lee Nickson, and Greg Nickson. Good friends like Jonathon and Judy Savill, Mike Murtagh, Paul Clark and Kathy Sorbo, Dennis Wilken, the lads at the George and Dragon who ensure my feet stay firmly on the ground at all times, the Leeds United mailing list for constant entertainment and erudition. Last, but very far from least, my wife Linda, and my son, Graham, who conspire to make every day a wonder and a joy.

I'm also indebted to the following sources for this book: ''Talking Pictures: Interviews with Contemporary British Filmmakers,'' edited by Lucy

Johnson (BFI Publishing); "Ewan McGregor" by Alan Jones; "Screwball With an Edge," by Kristine McKenna, *Los Angeles Times*, February 2, 1997; "On a Fast Track," by David Gritten, *Los Angeles Times*, July 21, 1997; "Tracking a Meteor from Scotland," by Jan Stuart, *Newsday*, June 1, 1997; "Ewan McGregor's Roles Are Varied," by Jack Garner, *Gannett News Service*, June 24, 1997; "*Trainspotting*'s Engine That Could" by Mark Jolly, *Interview*, August 1996; "The Next Brit Bright Star" by Richard Corliss, *Time*, July 15, 1996; "Ewan McGregor, Actor," by Ben Thompson, *Independent*, January 28, 1996; "Ewan McGregor," by Bill Van Parys; "Stupor Heroes from Scotland" by Jeff Gordinier, *Entertainment Weekly*, August 2, 1996; "Mod Couple" by Gerri Gallagher, *W*, September 1997; "Ordinary People" by Benjamin Svetkey, *Entertainment Weekly*, October 24, 1997; "Emm Fatale" by Marianne Gray, *Film Review*, October 1996; "Mad About the Boy," by Anwar Brett, *Film Review Special*, 1996; "Scottish Cinema" by Harlan Kennedy, *Film Comment*, July/August 1996; "May the 4th Be with You," by Steve Daly, *Entertainment Weekly*, June 13, 1997; "It Had to be Ewan" by Benjamin Svetkey, *Entertainment Weekly*, June 13, 1997; "Joined, Hiply" by John Clark, *Los Angeles Times*, October 19, 1997; "This One's Taken" by Sophie Wilson, *Sky International*, October 1997; "A Man of Many Parts" by Michael Dwyer, *Irish Times*, June 21, 1997; "Caledonian Supernova" by Ian Nathan, *Empire*, November 1997; "Off-Kilter" by John Brodie, *Premiere*, November 1997; "The Anticipation is Killing Me" by Phillipa Bloom, *Premiere* (UK), March 1996; "Trainspotting" by Caroline

Westbrook, *Empire*, March 1996; "Something Has Survived, Baby" by David Gritten, *Los Angeles Times*, July 27, 1997; "A Life More Ordinary" by Susan Wloszczyna, *USA Today*, October 24, 1997; "Dealing in Controversy" by David Gritten, *Daily Telegraph*, February 7, 1998; "Ewan McGregor: Straight Up" by Gavin Edwards, *Details*, November 1997; "Ewan McGregor" *People*, November 18, 1996; "A New Role for *Trainspotting* Star" by Jack Garner, *Gannett News Service*, May 14, 1997; "Pete Postlethwaite" by Richard Von Busack, *Metro*, May 29–June 4, 1997; "Super Brass" by Tim Fennell, *Sky International*, December 1996; "Blowing Her Own Trumpet" by Helen Barlow, *New Zealand Herald*, August 7, 1997; "The Boys are Back in Town" by Andrew O'Hagan, *Sight and Sound*, February 1996; "Now Arriving" by Louise Brealey, *Sky International*, May 1996; "Smokin' " by Louise Brealey, *Sky International*, May 1996.

Ewan

McGregor

Introduction

It's like this: A boy, living a life bounded by school and family, is fascinated with his uncle. His parents, everyone he knows, seem so ordinary. But the uncle is a free spirit. His hair is long, he dresses as he pleases, convention seems to mean nothing to him.

In a world where everything, even life itself, seems pre-ordained, it's natural that the boy would admire his uncle. The man has escaped. He's become bohemian, a bit of a hippie. He's also an actor, making his living by becoming other people, by *playing*. What boy wouldn't think of that as an ideal life?—even more so when he can go to the cinema and see his uncle onscreen in some of the defining films of the late twentieth century: the *Star Wars* trilogy.

Maybe it was inevitable that the boy would grow up and become an actor himself. Perhaps it was something in the genes, or that lingering boyhood fascination. Or perhaps it was an overriding desire to break away from the mundane life he saw stretching for years ahead of him.

Maybe the reasons don't matter as much as the fact that he did it—and with his parents' blessing. After an apprenticeship of sorts, he ended up at a prestigious drama school. Before he even had a chance to graduate, he was plucked from the ranks and slotted into a television series that was bound to get widespread critical attention, because of its writer, the controversial Dennis Potter.

Acting, they say, can be the hardest profession. So many spend most of their time "resting," either unemployed or as waiters, shop assistants, or anything that pays the bills. All the desire and the ability in the world means nothing without a healthy pinch of luck.

The boy—who'd grown to a handsome man now—turns out to have both talent *and* luck, the kind of combination that can be world-beating. He quickly ends up with a major part in a British film, and like a snowball rolling downhill, that leads to more and more, including the lead in *Trainspotting*, the apex of the British film industry for the nineties.

In its turn, that leads to more offers that just can't be refused, because he's a workaholic. Along the way he falls in love, marries, and becomes a father. It could almost be a fairy tale. This is a man who has everything he could possibly want from life.

He's in a remarkable position for an actor. Not only is he working constantly, but he's also able to combine art with commerce. He's not the biggest name at the multiplex, but he does seem to guarantee a certain level of integrity. He's vocal in his condemnation of Hollywood and everything it stands for. The big movie, which relies on special effects for its impact, is anathema to him. He doesn't understand the system, and he has no desire to become a part of it.

Even so . . .

There's one offer he simply can't turn down. It

brings everything full circle, and closes the first chapter of his life.

It's the call to go to another universe, far, far away. Not to take part in a blockbuster *du jour*, but something far more significant—the long-promised prequel to George Lucas's *Star Wars* trilogy. True, there'd be special effects galore, and yes, it would be entertainment on a massive scale. But this wasn't simply another Hollywood attempt to chase the consumer dollar. It would be *Star Wars*. It had been a defining moment for two generations—on its initial release in 1977, and then when it was re-released 20 years later. The next series of three would be a cultural milestone for the Millennium generation. Not so much a series of movies as an event that stood above and apart from anything else.

The original Obi Wan Kenobi, light saber ablaze, voice booming from his chest with years of stage-craft, was the venerable Alec Guinness. He would be a difficult act to follow, the personification of an aging Jedi Knight in his white beard and robes. But Lucas believed this was the man to do it. And how could the man betray a sacred trust like that? The Force was with him.

There would also be something more personal. The uncle who'd been the original inspiration, who'd even put acting into the man's mind as a possibility, had been one of the few actors to have roles in all three of the original *Star Wars* films. How could he turn down the opportunity to continue what had become a family tradition?

Of course, there would be a downside; there always was. It would push him into a place he really didn't enjoy—the intensely public glare of the spotlight. With the appearance of the film, his name would be on everyone's lips. He was already a star of sorts, but enough of a chameleon and actor that it was his *characters*, rather than the man himself, whom people thought they knew.

But *Star Wars* would vault him into an altogether different league, something beyond even his wildest imaginings. He'd had the lead roles in a number of films already, but he'd never portrayed someone who was already a cultural icon. Real, undeniable, honest-to-God stardom was waiting in 1999, and having taken on the part, he had to get used to the idea.

The boy (and the man), of course, is Ewan McGregor, who's become Scotland's biggest export since Sean Connery and the kilt. If there's one actor who typifies Britain in the nineties, it's Ewan. The actor as rock star, in a way. He can move from philosophizing junkie (*Trainspotting*) to inept action hero (*A Life Less Ordinary*) to rock star (*Velvet Goldmine*) to human canvas (*The Pillow Book*). He can go from art to commerce, and back again; from television to the big screen and even to the stage—and then all the way to the ultimate blockbuster. He can go where he wants, when he wants. He shows that acting ability doesn't have to be gained through endless productions of Shakespeare or an ego the size of the *Titanic*. Or even a superior attitude. Ewan McGregor is a regular guy, a normal bloke; he just happens to make his living acting in films.

The glamor and glitz associated with stardom hold no charm for him. He's not striving to make the A-list, to be seen with the right people in the right places. He makes his *living* from acting; that's very far from being his entire life.

There's no house in the Hollywood hills, not even a country estate in England. Instead, he lives in a decidedly untrendy part of north London. He's happily married, the father of a daughter. That's his real life.

In other words, forget any assumptions you might have made about the man from seeing his films. They're not *him*. They're his work. Unlike, say, Robert De Niro, Ewan doesn't live his characters. When he leaves the set each day, he leaves them behind, to be picked up again the next morning. There's no Method (and certainly no madness) to his work.

There is, however, an abundance of talent, which is what makes it so easy to believe he is all the people he's played, or that, somehow, they're him. The more prosaic truth is that he's a professional, with an uncanny knack to reach inside and bring these folk out as and when they're required. And it's also true that he's an unabashed workaholic, incapable of saying no to any project that interests him, even when it means squeezing an already full schedule even tighter. He loves his work, and just can't stop doing it. He's in that lucky position: the offers are coming to him—he doesn't have to pursue them. He loves being in films.

"I think making films is brilliant," he said. "Going on location is amazing, hanging about with all these film people doing their thing."

So is Ewan McGregor an enigma?

The simple answer is: No more than anybody else. He's not particularly broody or moody, he doesn't approach life with an attitude. Quite the opposite. It's there to be embraced in all its facets. There's joy to be had both at work and home.

Ewan knows he's lucky. He's in the kind of position most actors only dream about. Right now the biggest question is how the celebrity of his *Star Wars* role will affect him professionally. In a way, up until this, he's operated slightly under the radar. He's been viewed as an actor, rather than a celebrity, a star.

But the three films that will comprise the *Star Wars* prequel are going to be huge; there can be no doubt of that, and no escaping it. Ewan will be a million plastic figures played with by boys and girls all over the world. His face will look down from posters on bedroom walls. Like it or not, he'll be elevated to an image. Things are going to change.

The only actor whose long-term career benefitted from (or survived, depending on your point of view) the first *Star Wars* trilogy was Harrison Ford. He's gone on to become a major star. As to the others—Mark Hamill, Carrie Fisher—*Star Wars* was really the high point of their cinematic careers.

But when those films appeared, the cult of personality that seems to rule the film industry today didn't exist in the same way. If anything, it congregated around directors, people like Lucas and Spielberg, rather than actors. These days, however, it's all about Star Power. And Ewan's star quotient is about to go through the roof.

Then again, to many people it seemed like he became a star overnight. After a very heavily featured role in *Shallow Grave*, the film that put Scotland back on the map, he seemed to be everywhere—in a version of Stendhal's classic *The Red and the Black* on British television, followed in rapid succession by big screen appearances in *Trainspotting* (where, as Renton, the central character, he completely stole the show), *The Pillow Book*, and *Emma*, yet another adaptation of a Jane Austen novel. And truthfully, he had film stacked up like planes waiting to land at a busy airport. It was almost as if he was trying to win the title of the hardest-working man in show business.

For an actor, however, the biggest thing is getting the chance to play the parts. So many attend auditions hopefully and go away crushed that the chances Ewan had were impossible to refuse. And it wasn't as if Ewan was in any danger of being typecast. He'd moved from yuppie journalist to drug addict, to human book and aristocrat and beyond. To play Renton in *Trainspotting* he lost twenty-eight pounds, then quickly regained the weight for his next role.

If he's difficult to pin down, it's because he doesn't pin himself down as an actor. Unlike so many in Hollywood who hit on a winning character and spend their entire careers playing variations on it, the essence of acting for Ewan is its variety and constant challenge.

"I hope I won't do just any film to become a star. I just want to carry on working, acting."

He could relive his adolescent music fantasies (as a teenager he was actually in a band, called Scarlet Pride) by playing an "Iggy Pop-type" person in Todd Haynes's exploration of the glam-rock scene, *Velvet Goldmine*, then find himself where the six-year-old Ewan dreamed of being—in outer space, with all the magic of the Force. More than that, he could get paid for doing it—although the money is hardly that of "major" Hollywood names. What more could a person ask of life?

From work, very little. And he's learning more

every day about his own limits. He began with none—he was young, hopeful, and he was willing to give anything a shot. Now he knows a little more, and he's coming to terms with his own limitations, some of which were shown when he tried to play an American in *Nightwatch* (which was released in 1998, but actually was filmed before 1997's *A Life Less Ordinary*).

But somehow Ewan and America haven't been a perfect fit. Not in terms of popularity, but the man and the place. He's been quite vocal in his opposition to the way the business works in Hollywood, and he seems far happier in Europe than in the United States.

And that's fine; not everything is for everybody. But the unvarnished fact is that Ewan is going to become a household name. Not just in Europe, or the rest of the world, but most particularly in America, where two generations have been eagerly awaiting the prequels to *Star Wars* and his portrayal of Obi Wan.

So what exactly has led up to this? Who is Ewan McGregor? What has he done? Has he really lived a life that's been less ordinary?

One

Like most places in Britain, Crieff has a long, convoluted history. In the county of Perthshire, in Scotland, it stands at the crossroads of what today are known as the A85 and the A822, not too far from the internationally famous Gleneagles golf course. The nearest town of any real size is Perth, some thirty miles to the east. Glasgow and Edinburgh aren't that far away, maybe an hour to the south by road, but culturally they could be in another country altogether.

Crieff stands on the edge of the Scottish lowlands. At one time it was probably the northernmost town where English was the common language; go any farther and you were surrounded by Gaelic speakers as you ventured into the Highlands.

The town has been burned to the ground once, and almost a second time (in revenge for its progovernment sympathies during Scottish uprisings). It was the center of the county of Perthshire at one point, a thriving market town, where Highland farmers brought their cattle to the famous cattle market. Bonnie Prince Charlie reviewed his beaten troops there for one last time in 1746 after his rebellion against the English Crown had been defeated.

During the Victorian era Crieff shook off the wildness of its past and became respectable. Morrisons Academy, a famous boarding school, opened for business in 1859. The Hydro, the kind of spa hotel so loved by that generation for its supposedly health-giving waters, was built in 1869. And in 1872, Crieff even began to look nostalgically to its past with the first of the Highland Games, where the Scots did in competition what they had once done in work and anger.

The town became genteel, a place of public propriety, with private lives concealed behind net curtains. The Drummonds and Murrays, once the warring clans of the area, were now prosperous gentleman farmers.

In the twentieth century, little changed. Maybe it didn't have quite the prosperity it once had, but Crieff wasn't a shabby, poverty-stricken relative, either. It remained a good Presbyterian place, full of the old values, with little time for the quicker pace of living that was consuming the rest of the world. Hard work, a good appearance, and a belief in a stern God could easily have been its watchwords, barely changed over the course of a hundred years.

This was where Ewan Gordon McGregor was born, on March 31, 1971, in the place he said was full of "haggis and heather." His father, James, was on the staff at Morrisons Academy, doubling as a physical education teacher and career advisor. Ewan was the family's second son.

For all Crieff's conservatism, it was a good place for a growing boy. It was small and safe, free from the crime and violence that seemed to become endemic to British cities in the seventies. The young

Ewan could vanish into the nearby countryside with his friends for the day without worry.

"You know, spending all day with your mates, with catapults and stuff, getting up to no good. It was great. I had a brilliant time."

The McGregors were an ordinary family. They worked hard, and had aspirations for their boys. One advantage of James McGregor's job was that the lads could be educated for free at Morrisons, although they'd be day students (in other words, they would return home after classes) rather than boarders. It was a fine distinction of class, but nonetheless, it meant they'd both go into the world with not only a superior education, but also some influential contacts through their classmates.

It was a very settled, ordered existence for the family. At least it was until Ewan's uncle (his mother's brother) would come and visit.

Denis Lawson was an actor, who lived in London and worked on television, stage, and films. He was, really, the black sheep of the family—the one who'd rejected convention—and that made him an impossibly exotic figure to young Ewan.

"I remember throughout my childhood in the seventies, he used to come and see us and he'd always look really different from other people I knew," Ewan recalled. "He had flares on and sideburns and beads and a big sheepskin waistcoat and didn't wear any shoes, and I wanted to be just like him."

It wasn't that the acting bug struck early—at five Ewan didn't understand what an actor did—but it was more the sense of being different, of breaking the mold, that appealed to him, an appeal that would only get stronger as time passed.

Lawson was a hippie, and to a boy surrounded by stultifying Scottish conservatism and the *thou shalt not*s of the Presbyterian church, Lawson's lifestyle—lived in London, no less!—was immediately attractive.

That only increased when Lawson was cast in what might have been the most influential movie of the decade—*Star Wars*. Granted, as Wedge, an X-Wing fighter pilot, he didn't exactly have one of the leading roles, but he was there, a part of film history, and he'd be featured in the entire trilogy.

Ewan was six when the film arrived at his local cinema in 1977. "I remember standing outside school waiting to be picked up, so excited."

It was impossible not to be caught up in the film. As Ewan would say later, looking back as an adult, "They're just little fairy stories, really, there's not a great deal going on. . . . They go from here, and they get stuck here. . . . There's a fight there, and then they end up here."

But it was David and Goliath, good against evil, Cowboys and Indians, Saturday morning cliffhanger series, all neatly wrapped up in a futuristic package and tied with the most amazing and realistic special effects anyone had ever seen. It was its own universe, and it was impossible not to want to go there—especially when your uncle was involved in it all.

It had an effect on him, but in the way of kids, so did a lot of other things, particularly if Uncle Denis was involved.

"When I watched him on the [television] or on the stage I was just so mesmerized that this guy— my uncle—was doing that, it fascinated me."

A year after *Star Wars,* Ewan fell in love with

Grease, and spent a year crossing and recrossing his fingers, hoping that Olivia Newton-John would somehow magically appear in his classroom. Not too surprisingly, she didn't, but Ewan did go so far as to try and restage the song "You're the One that I Want" in the playground, with himself in the Travolta role.

Films were rapidly taking a bigger part in his life. And not only the newest releases.

"Saturday and Sundays would be old black-and-white movies back-to-back," he recalled. "Old romances from Hollywood and Ealing from the forties and fifties. Jimmy Stewart movies, stuff like that."

His love of the movies and the way they could sweep him away, as well as his desire to emulate his bohemian uncle, combined to give him the desire to become an actor himself. By the age of nine his mind was made up, "and I wouldn't let anyone sway me."

The initial spark of interest, he realized later, had actually come at a much earlier age, from the British tradition known as pantomime. Staged every Christmas in theaters, often starring people well-known in fields apart from acting, they retold classic fairy tales in hilarious fashion, for kids, with plenty of audience participation. There were comical villains, and always a lovely young woman, in a short costume, playing the male lead.

"Remember the principal boy was always played by a woman?" Ewan asked in *Empire*. "It all became about legs and I fell in love with the leading ladies. So, it had a lot to do with sex."

There was a great difference between being nine and deciding to become something and actually doing it as an adult. For a start, Ewan had no idea *how* to become an actor. And it wasn't his sole focus in life. He was young, a boy, with interests all over the place. Living so close to the country, he loved to ride, although the McGregors couldn't afford to buy him a horse. So he did the next best thing, and exchanged work for riding time at a local stable, going in every weekend and mucking out the stalls to earn the freedom to be on horseback.

Roaming and riding in the countryside was one thing; the four walls of a classroom were another. As the sons of a teacher, both Ewan and his older brother were under a lot of pressure to do well at Morrisons Academy. Not only was it their ticket to a good life, but they had to uphold the family name. For the elder McGregor boy, it seemed to come naturally. He achieved the distinction of being named head boy (the closest American equivalent would be valedictorian), and would go on to become a fighter pilot in the Royal Air Force.

Ewan was about as different from him as chalk from cheese. He wasn't particularly trying to be rebellious or awkward; it was just the way things seemed to be.

"I wasn't interested in school. I got into trouble all the time and they kept saying: Attitude problem. I was unaware I had one because I had one, and it was starting to embarrass my father."

By the time Ewan was in his teens it was apparent that he and school were never going to become the best of friends. It was the eighties. The whole punk scene of music had been and gone, leaving little except short spiky hair, some fashion sense, and a breath of fresh musical air that was soon overcome by smog.

Like so many teenage boys, Ewan was taken by music. When he was younger, he'd had a poster of Elvis (Presley, not Costello) on his bedroom wall, a man who seemed to him to bridge the gap between music and film. For a while, Ewan wanted to be Elvis. But as he grew, and his tastes changed, he came to realize he could make his own music.

And that was exactly what he did.

He switched music heroes from Elvis to Billy Idol, formerly the singer for Generation X, and now a solo artist with hits like ''White Wedding'' and ''Rebel Yell.'' He learned to play the drums and joined a band called Scarlet Pride. He'd put red paint in his hair to color it—teenage boys in Crieff didn't understand the finer points of hair dye—and tied red bandanas around the knees of his jeans.

The fact that Scarlet Pride wasn't particularly good (or that Ewan wasn't a natural drummer, by any means) didn't matter; he was doing something. It was like acting, in its own way, putting on a persona for an audience, copping an attitude, being a star for a few moments, being anyone but Ewan Gordon McGregor, Crieff schoolboy. Rock'n'roll wasn't his only musical outlet, however. At school Ewan had taken up the French horn (and would make his first major public appearance, on Scottish television as a teenager, playing it).

At the same time he was playing in a band, Ewan was also becoming a . . . golfer. It might have seemed at odds with the ideas of rock'n'roll and acting, but this was Scotland, where the game had been invented, and, as he pointed out, ''In Scotland, there's not the same elitist thing with golf. We used to play a lot on public courses, just for something to do. When I was fourteen, I got thrown off a golf course for swearing. After every shot I would get really angry, screaming ... Eventually this guy drove up in a tractor and told me I had to leave because the other golfers had been complaining. So I had to walk back in shame with my clubs. I didn't play for a long time after that. ... I just got fed up."

The center of his thoughts, and his desire for the future, though, remained acting. Everything else was for show, or a way to pass the endless time in a sleepy Scottish town. It had all received a boost in 1983, the year Ewan turned twelve, when a Scottish film opened. *Local Hero* was written and directed by Bill Forsyth, who'd made his reputation two years earlier with *Gregory's Girl*. More importantly, apart from the legendary Burt Lancaster, veteran of so many of those black-and-white films that had filled Ewan's weekends, one of the stars was his uncle, Denis Lawson.

Set in contemporary Scotland, *Local Hero* presented something that Ewan could not only relate to, but also with which he could empathize. Films could have something do with with life as he understood it.

Now there was no doubt that he wanted to act. The only question, still, was how he could go about doing it.

None of this helped him with his schoolwork, much to the disappointment of his parents. After watching one son sail through Morrisons, now the other one was close to drowning.

"I became quite depressed, I've been told, and started getting into trouble all the time," Ewan said. It wasn't exactly the reputation a respected teacher wanted for his son. More importantly, it wasn't good for Ewan. He wasn't happy there, but he would have been unhappy in almost any school. The academic life just wasn't right for him. The only subjects he cared about were music and art, neither of which was considered "academic" enough for Morrisons; so that outlet was thwarted. What was particularly worrying was that he didn't seem to notice his own depression, or the fact that he seemed to be causing trouble; it wasn't something he deliberately set out to do. He was just kicking out, trying to forge his own life, and school, particularly Morrisons, which placed such emphasis on academic achievement, wasn't the place to do it.

It all came to a head when he was sixteen. Things were sliding from bad to worse, and he wasn't even aware of it. All he knew was what was expected of him—learning, exams, eventually the Highers, and finally university. The road seemed to stretch ahead of him for years, well beyond the horizon.

The turning point, he remembered, was a dark night, the rain coming down heavily. He was driving into town with his parents.

"I've spoken to your father," his mother began, "and you are going to be an actor. That's what you always wanted to do. You don't need to stay for your exams. You are depressed, and you should get out."

In many ways, it was the only thing they could do, either that or watch Ewan suffer through at least two more years of school, becoming even more unhappy. For years he'd made no secret of his ultimate wish to act, even though he'd done little about it—no amateur dramatics, no school plays.

"It's not always an easy thing to be told by your son, 'I'm going to be an actor,'" Ewan said. "I don't think it was an easy thing for them to hear but they were always right behind me.''

One of the things that made it even harder for Mr. and Mrs. McGregor was already having an actor in the family. Ewan might have had a romantic view of his Uncle Denis's life, but his parents knew the reality of an actor's life, ''that Denis went through years and years of hard stuff.''

His dream was going to come true. Ewan was going to be an actor. Now he had to start asking the hard questions, like how would he do it?

Two

The answer was, by learning the craft from the ground up. That was the way many people had started, and it was going to be Ewan's grounding, too. Unless you knew the right people, you didn't drop out of school and suddenly find yourself in movies.

Crieff was too small a town to boast a professional theater. The nearest was in Perth, the city that was the heart of Tayside. So, at sixteen, Ewan found a room in a boarding house in Perth and began work at Perth Theatre as an assistant stage manager, a fancy title for someone who had to do anything and everything that needed to be done, from cleaning to selling tickets—most of the lowly jobs.

"I had left home and was working in the theater as a scene changer. I didn't know what acting was. As far as I knew, it was remembering words."

Obviously, there was still an awful lot left to learn, and the first lesson came a week after he began his career. Perth Theatre was staging *A Passage to India*, and Ewan found himself onstage during the production as a supernumerary (extra). It was an experience unlike any other he'd had. It wasn't like being in a band, but part of something much bigger. And he liked it. In fact, suddenly he liked everything about life.

"I learned an awful lot about life and growing, because I hadn't really seen anything before. I met gay people and I met people who were having affairs. I gobbled it all up—it was brilliant."

What he understood very quickly, however, was that being an assistant stage manager, with its endless hours and paltry pay, wasn't going to teach him much about acting. Shifting scenery was all well and good, but it didn't seem likely to help him reach his dream. For that he'd need drama school.

It was, perhaps, the first time the idea of school had excited him. But then again, if he was accepted, he'd be going of his own volition, to learn something that was important to him.

He sat down with his parents and explained what he wanted to do. They were right behind him, even though they'd have to pay for this education—there would be no grants or scholarships. They were just pleased to see their son want to do something constructive, to have him happy again. They were willing to make sacrifices, and in the end even sold some of their things to help Ewan continue his education.

The most immediate help came, of course, from Uncle Denis, who came to visit as Ewan was preparing for his audition. If he passed, he'd become a student at Kirkcaldy Drama School, on their one-year course. It was hardly the Royal Academy of Dramatic Art, but Ewan wasn't ready for somewhere like that. Not yet. Kirkcaldy, fifty miles away on Scotland's east coast, just a hop, skip, and a jump from Edinburgh and Glasgow, seemed much more real.

The closest thing to a stage Ewan and Denis could find for rehearsals was the school gym at Morrisons Academy, so that was where they went, "[a]nd I was doing a scene for him in the school gym, a monologue for an English skinhead, and I was going like this and this, with no anger. And my uncle stopped me and said, 'Remember when you got beaten up in Glasgow, those guys that punched you in the head, kicked you in the ground, and you looked like a wimp? C'mon, start swearing.'"

Quite suddenly, Ewan was finding something in himself that he'd never known existed. He was in another place, "standing on the table shouting a blue streak. Then the janitor walked into the gym and said, 'What's going on?'"

The lesson reached an abrupt end, but at that point it didn't matter. Ewan had learned something very important, how to tap into his own power and make his words come alive.

Ewan passed the audition with flying colors, and before he was seventeen, he'd moved for a second time, down to Kirkcaldy.

For a boy from a small town, it was perfect—smaller than Perth, easily negotiable, and not too expensive. If he wanted big city life, Edinburgh was less than an hour away by train or bus. He was on his own, with more freedom than he'd enjoyed in Perth, not being tied to a job which kept him at the theater for endless hours, although he did earn a little money by washing dishes in a restaurant.

Kirkcaldy Drama School, like most places in Scotland, was without pretension. That was just as well. For someone who'd been so much in love with acting, Ewan came in with hardly any knowledge. The power that his uncle had helped him tap into was instinctive. That was fine, but it was raw. He needed to learn how to channel it, to use it professionally. And there was plenty more to be learned too, beginning with the very basics of memorizing and understanding lines, marks (where to stand on the stage)—in short, everything.

Luckily, being a student at drama school was very different from being a day pupil at Morrisons Academy. There was little formality, no uniforms, and a relatively lax discipline. The boy who, just a year before, had been getting into trouble, was transformed into the model of learning.

In fact, he was drinking it all in. This was all stuff he'd ached to know, things he was eager to commit to memory. He'd thrown himself into all this not even knowing if he really could act, let alone *how* to act. He realized very quickly—as did his teachers—that he had a huge natural talent, an ability to transform himself into the characters he was playing and make them real flesh-and-blood people, not just lines someone had written. Everything else, all the mechanics and techniques, were things that could be learned.

And he was acquiring that learning at a remarkable speed. It was something of a new sensation for him, being eager to get to classes and being attentive. The big thrill, though, came in performances, when he could put what he'd been taught into practice, and marry it to the power inside himself.

Kirkcaldy was hardly a famous drama school; it had never produced any stars, more the jobbing actors who tended to stay at a lower level, mostly unknown but working consistently—the backbone of the profession, rather than its brightest lights.

It was apparent that Ewan wasn't destined to become just another jobbing actor. His teachers knew that before he did. To Ewan, he was just doing what came naturally, and getting a grounding in the basics. To an observer, his talent eclipsed all those around him. He was someone who could make it, who had the range and the rare quality that could make him a standout.

The problem was that his talent was too big for Kirkcaldy. What they could teach him wasn't going to stretch him and help him make the most of himself. After a few months it was already being suggested that Ewan apply somewhere else for a full, three-year course.

As an idea, it was all well and good. But where? RADA, the Royal Academy of Dramatic Art, was a possibility, the obvious one, with its great reputation. And it was Ewan's first choice. He applied, and was given an audition.

That meant traveling to London on the train, as well as spending another 30 pounds—the fee RADA charged just to let a potential student audition for them. So he'd already spent one hundred pounds (approximately $150) with no guarantee of a place. But if he was accepted, he figured it would be worth every penny.

He was a little surprised to arrive and find only one man in an office waiting for him. He'd expected a group of three or four, enough to judge him properly. His monologues were prepared, as required—one Shakespeare and one contemporary. Instead of starting the audition, however, the man asked him to sit down, so they could begin with a chat.

"How old are you?" he asked. Seventeen, was Ewan's reply.

"Ah, you've got a good few years of auditions ahead of you yet."

At that point Ewan realized he wasn't going to get a place at RADA, and it rankled that the proper opportunity had never been given to him—it still rankles to this day. That left what had originally been his second choice, the Guildhall School of Music and Drama.

Like the Royal Academy, it was situated in London, a country—a world, really—away from Crieff or Kirkcaldy. For a kid of seventeen, it would be a huge dislocation, to be on his own in a huge city, four hundred miles from home, in a place where people ostensibly spoke the same language, but with utterly different accents and idioms. This wasn't even Edinburgh, but the English capital, where, it seemed, it all happened. It was where Uncle Denis had gone to make his fortune. It was the center of show business in Britain. The big theaters were there. The British movie industry, such as it was, was based there. If Ewan was going to make his living as an actor, he'd have to move there eventually. Why not do it now, when he'd be learning, rather than hoping to find a job?

First, however, he had to pass the audition. He was a shining student at Kirkcaldy, but competition for places at Guildhall was much tougher. Once again Denis Lawson helped him prepare his monologues. The boy had come a long way in a very short time, but there was still an awful lot to learn. If he could get a place at the school, he'd be able to prove to himself and to everyone else that he really was going places, that he wasn't just another sullen drop-out who couldn't find a real job in the poor Scottish economy.

He worked long and hard getting ready, at home, and again with his uncle in London. This was the big one. His teachers had told him he had a natural gift for acting; this would be the acid test.

He passed. As of September 1989, Ewan Mc-Gregor would be living south of the border, down among the Sassenachs, as the Scots called the English.

The Guildhall School of Music and Drama wasn't the most prestigious of Britain's acting schools. Its most famous alumni tended to be classical musicians. But it is still a solid institution where Ewan could expand his knowledge of theater, of acting, and of the world in general.

Founded in 1880, the Guildhall School, located on Silk Street, now formed part of the Barbican Arts complex that had developed on the edge of the old City of London. There were theaters, a conference center, the school, everything all together.

It was an odd district. Around the school, in the city, there was plenty of money and history. A few blocks away were remains of London's original Roman wall, a reminder that the city had been around for virtually two thousand years. A little to the south was the financial heart of the place, where millions were made and lost every day. But less than half a mile to the east was Spitalfields, once the site of a famous market, and the start of the East End, home of the Cockneys. A walk along Bethnal Green Road could take Ewan from one world into another, from privilege to people just struggling to get by. The East End had always been a working-class area. Violence lurked under the surface, and sometimes it broke through, as in the Kray twins, the gangsters who became local heroes and virtually ruled the area back in the 1960s.

But this was the late eighties. Ten years of Conservative rule under Margaret Thatcher had had an effect on everyone. The rich were richer, and the poor were decidedly poorer. Unemployment was rife, particularly in working-class areas. Many East Enders had worked on the River Thames, in the many docks that had comprised the Port of London. Almost every dock had now closed.

By contrast, going to the Guildhall, working at what he'd always desired and feeling fulfilled, Ewan must have felt positively bourgeois. And he was, really. His parents didn't have the kind of money that could be made wheeling and dealing in the city, but he'd grown up in the middle class, relatively privileged, and never wanting for anything.

The school was everything he'd hoped it would be. Kirkcaldy had been great, but it was never going to stretch him. Here people would push him to find his limits and expand them. He could advance his technique, learn more plays, and get more experience performing. He could also learn by watching others perform. The West End, with its theater district along Shaftesbury Avenue, was just a short ride away on the Tube. South of the River was the Young Vic, where he could see all manner of productions on the stage.

Then there were all the bands that played London, big shows, performances in clubs—all perfect for a boy who'd never quite outgrown rock'n'roll, and who never would. London itself became a playground, the sinful square blocks of Soho, with strip clubs, prostitutes, and bars—a place that still holds some of his favorite pubs. From Crieff, which had nothing, he'd come to the center of the world, where it was all laid out before him. He loved the place with all its variety. And during the long summer breaks he could head back to Scotland.

"[W]hen I was in drama school I used to work on farms in the holiday and that was hard work. It was quite good to work with [your head] all the time and then to go away and work with your arms ... I worked on a fishfarm once, and I was a car valet. I used to polish BMWs."

The course lasted three years. Like any student, there were classes he loved, and others he loathed. There was one course in particular, all improvisation, that became like therapy to him, a way to get in touch with himself, and learn how to bring out that innate talent. But he hated being taught the Method—made famous by actors like Marlon Brando, James Dean, and Robert De Niro—where the actor literally became his character for as long as he was playing it. That went far beyond acting; that intruded into real life, and what was the point in that?

Ewan wasn't trying to be the best student ever to emerge from the Guildhall. All he really eventually wanted from life was to work as hard and as often as he could. He had no illusions about stardom. It happened to a lucky few, and he really didn't care if he was among that feted elite, as long as the roles kept coming thick and fast, enough to satisfy the drive to perform that was in him.

"I'm so driven," he admitted, "working madly,

and almost arrogantly ambitious. But I've never known towards where or what.''

The most immediate where and what took place in his final year. The senior students always put on an open evening, giving them a chance to perform and show their stuff to the agents and casting directors who'd appear and try to spot the upcoming talent.

In January 1992, Ewan was part of the group preparing for the show. He'd be performing two songs and two monologues, an opportunity to show his versatility.

''And it's the scariest thing in the world,'' he said. To open, he'd chosen, of all things, a Barbra Streisand song, with some dancing—not something most fans would ever associate with Ewan McGregor—which he called ''a terrible . . . number,'' before moving on to something more soulful, his version of Bill Withers's 1970s hit, ''Lean On Me.'' It was catchy, poppy, enough, he remembered, that ''we were singing it for weeks after.''

He'd managed to survive the first part of the program, what should have been the roughest part. Although he had a reasonable voice, singing wasn't his forte, certainly not compared to acting, which he'd get to do later in the evening.

After an intermission, it was time for him to return to the stage, and he began by performing the ''Fork it!'' speech from *Withnail & I*, the 1987 film (coproduced by George Harrison and Ringo Starr) that had been something of a cultural landmark of British cinema. That went well, and now there was only one thing left—the monologue he'd written himself, in which he played an oil worker who'd lost his legs in an accident on one of the North Sea rigs.

He pushed himself onto the middle of the stage in a wheelchair, his legs tucked uncomfortably under him, and began to speak. Then the actor's nightmare happened. Right in the middle of the showcase, the thing that could give his budding professional career a massive boost, he forgot his lines. He did the only thing he could think of, turned silent, looked down, and rubbed his stump until his memory returned.

"And I came off and I thought, 'That's it, I've blown it.' And then I found out that I hadn't, much to my surprise."

Quite the opposite, it seemed. At least one person in the audience had been very impressed with the way Ewan handled himself on the stage that night. He was a talent scout from Channel 4, who thought that this lad might be perfect for a new series that was currently being cast.

Lipstick on Your Collar was the latest offering from playwright Dennis Potter, the remarkable and unique talent who'd done so much to revolutionize television drama in England with series like *The Singing Detective* (which would eventually be shown in the United States), and *Pennies from Heaven*, which would be remade in 1981 in a watered-down Hollywood version as a vehicle for comedian Steve Martin.

After the show, the talent scout came and talked to Ewan, and casually mentioned the new project. Might he be interested? In appearing on television, in a Dennis Potter work? Was this serious, was this real? Was this a dream or some sort of wind-up? It was the kind of thing student actors could only dream about.

But the man from Channel 4 was completely serious. Ewan would be perfect for one of the roles. There was only one drawback. The casting was happening now, and filming was about to begin. If Ewan accepted, and passed the audition, he'd have to make himself available immediately, which would be difficult since he still had six months left until graduation.

That was going to be a hard decision. But first things first. He might not pass the audition, in which case the matter would be irrelevant.

He went to the studio and performed for the camera, reading from the script. He was exactly what they wanted. It would be a strongly featured role, just what a young unknown needed to get him started along the acting path.

Given the filming schedule, there was no way he could juggle the work with school. It was crunch time. Should he abandon the Guildhall, kiss almost three years of work goodbye—four if you counted Kirkcaldy—and his diploma? Should he hold his breath and plunge into the icy waters of professional acting?

He knew what he had to do. He'd got into all this in the first place because he wanted to act professionally. Now he was being given that chance, and he'd be a fool to turn down something this prestigious. A little reluctantly, but still smiling inside, Ewan said goodbye to the Guildhall School. His real life was just beginning.

Three

Lipstick on Your Collar didn't send Ewan spiralling straight to fame. He wasn't the show's star—that was Giles Thomas, playing Private Francis Francis—but he did enjoy a prominent role in the six-part series.

It took place in 1956, a year that was something of a turning point in British military and social history. In Egypt, the Suez crisis was underway.

Egypt had nationalized the Suez Canal, the waterway that linked the Mediterranean and the Red Sea. Britain took affront at that, perhaps because it had once been the colonial master of the region. With the help of France and Israel, in October the Conservative Prime Minister, Anthony Eden, began secret moves to invade and occupy the entire Suez Canal Zone.

It proved to be a strategy that was unpopular all over the world. Even America turned against its old ally. There were threats to the British currency, and the United Nations formally censured Britain, leaving the troops with no option but to withdraw. For a country that had once ruled fully one-quarter of the world, and been able to do anything it liked with virtual impunity, this was a shameful defeat, a sign that the pendulum really had swung the other way.

But there were more than political changes happening in Britain. After World War II, which had depleted resources and material, Britain had stayed austere and rationed until 1952. Now, though, prosperity was finally catching up. And so was the first real music for youths—rock'n'roll. Like America, the country had its first really separate teenage generation.

Rock'n'roll had gotten a toehold in the U.S. a couple of years earlier, with Elvis Presley's first records, quickly followed by Bill Haley, Little Richard, Jerry Lee Lewis, Chuck Berry, until it had become an unstoppable musical avalanche that changed the entire musical landscape.

England, a couple of years behind, came to rock 'n'roll by the back door, through skiffle: stripped-down, acoustic rock played on acoustic guitars and tea-chest basses, inspired largely by black American artists like Leadbelly. Lonnie Donegan had a hit single with a version of the traditional "Rock Island Line" that inspired a generation (including a young John Lennon and Paul McCartney) to pick up guitars.

From there, it was only a matter of time until real rock'n'roll caught the young ears, and the battle was over; rock won. But in 1956 it was still new, vital, and rebellious.

That was the background to *Lipstick on Your Collar*. Privates Francis Francis (Giles Thomas) and Mick Hopper (Ewan) both worked for a military intelligence bureau in London. Francis, living with his aunt and uncle in an apartment, was in love with their upstairs neighbor, Sylvia (Louise Germaine), and dreamed about saving her from her abusive husband—who just happened to be Francis's superior at work.

Hopper was Francis's best friend, and a dreamer himself. But his dreams revolved around music, and becoming a drummer in a rock'n'roll band (at least Ewan had had the practical experience for that from his time with Scarlet Pride); he was the one who'd suddenly break into song, jumping onto a table and lip-synching to Elvis Presley and starting in on a dance routine, a jive or a jitterbug.

"*Lipstick* is the story of two young men," said playwright Potter. "It is the story of a nation at a moment in crisis. It is the story of change, and the music is illustrating living in the change.... those two young actors—Ewan McGregor as Hopper, Giles Thomas as Francis—are played so well that I 'remembered' more and more as the production went on."

That was praise indeed, and it meant a lot, given that Potter had become one of the most innovative and respected television writers in Britain. This would be his last series, however, and in 1996 he would die.

Ewan actually spent some time with Potter, although being in public with him wasn't always easy.

"He was an embarrassing man to go to restaurants with," Ewan said, "very impatient and rude to waiters." But he was willing to offer advice to a young man just starting out.

"I'll never forget it. We were doing a scene in a graveyard, and he came and sat down with me. I'd just had my twenty-first birthday on the set, and he said, 'When this comes out, you'll be offered loads of stuff, and you mustn't take the first thing that comes along. Take the things that come from your gut.' And in the middle of this he'd get up, run off, throw up behind a gravestone [Potter was terminally ill]. It didn't break his stride. He'd just carry on, a man who had been ill for twenty years of his life.''

For his first professional engagement, Ewan had taken part not just in a show, but a true cultural event. It was a critical success, even if it was the kind of piece that would never find a mainstream commercial audience. It had given him his first taste of what it really meant to be an actor. He loved it, and he knew he'd made the right decision.

He would work on a posthumous Dennis Potter production, *Karaoke*, a couple of years later, in 1996. By then Ewan would be a big star, but he hadn't forgotten his debt to the man, taking a cameo in the mini-series.

''I didn't ever have to do those struggling years,'' he admitted. ''I'm not guilty about it anyway, a lot of actors want you to feel guilty about that. I didn't get the job to be unemployed and I've learned a lot from every job I've done since.''

Lipstick on Your Collar didn't translate into instant fame, as Ewan had briefly imagined it would.

''I thought that when the first episode of *Lipstick* was aired my life would change dramatically. I remember counting the days to the first transmission. But when it was screened nothing happened. Nobody recognized me. I didn't get mobbed. It was a huge anticlimax.''

Nor did it even immediately translate into another job. Ewan didn't think he was God's gift to the profession, but he did feel—without trying to be too cocky—that he was better than many who were getting roles that should have gone to him, as he spent a total of four months going from audition to audition.

"I dealt with it really badly and should have shut my mouth," he admitted. "But it's like anything: you're the one living this thing, so if you're pissed off at the time, you're pissed off. And you always think you'll never work again."

In Britain, unlike the U.S., actors tend to move smoothly back and forth between television and film; one isn't necessarily seen as a higher medium than the other. Great scripts occur in both, and the bottom line is that they both offer paying work. Ewan's second job saw him making the transition to the big screen, and during the summer of 1992 he went to North Africa for a small part in *Being Human*.

It was a comedy written and directed by Bill Forsyth, the Scot who ten years earlier had directed Ewan's Uncle Denis in *Local Hero*. This was an ambitious vehicle for Robin Williams, a risk that, if it paid off, would extend his already wide comedic range.

In the end, its reach was greater than its grasp; there were moments of humor and reflection, but it was *too* ambitious and unfocused to succeed properly.

For Ewan, however, it was a blast. He only had one line, but still got to travel and spend a lot of time partying.

"I spent a month dossing in Morocco to do one line," he recalled. "Fantastic: 'I'll do it, Don Paolo,' in a thick Glasgow accent." However, he seemed to have given more thought to the fun than the work, perhaps because he was still young and far from home, in another country for the first time. "I can remember the night before asking another actor, 'Are you going to do it in Scots?' Stupid, the *night* before I had my big day."

Well, perhaps not a *big* day, given that his entire contribution as the character Alvarez was that one line, but big enough in his own eyes. It was another credit to add to his resume.

Once that was done, and his Moroccan vacation complete, it was home to London, and his next job—he wasn't coming back to the unemployment line. London, however, was little more than a stopover, time to change clothes and head off again—this time to France.

Seemingly without trying, Ewan was rapidly making an impression, enough to be cast in a BBC adaptation of Stendhal's classic French novel, *The Red and the Black*, renamed *Scarlet and Black*. And it wasn't just any part, either, but Julien Sorel, the lead, a young man from the country who attempts first to make his way in the Church, then, when that doesn't advance him socially, undertakes to enter society by the seduction of aristocratic women.

It had been filmed before, a French production in 1954, which had starred Gerard Philipe, but this version, to be aired in three parts, was aimed much more at the *Masterpiece Theatre* crowd. To be fair, it was the kind of period piece the English had a reputation for doing superbly—authentic, lively, and superbly acted.

For Ewan, with three radically different parts in his first year as an actor, the diversity was part of the fun. "That's what it's all about, that's what keeps it interesting. I don't understand actors who don't see it that way. It's about working on different characters, portraying different people.''

Lipstick on Your Collar had given him a first chance to shine, but in many ways his performance had been overshadowed by the fact that it was a Dennis Potter teleplay. The script itself was the real star of the proceedings, rather than any of the actors. His performance in *Being Human* might as well not have even been there. This was going to be his first real test. Ewan not only made three hours of Stendhal entertaining, he made it thrilling viewing for a lot of people in Britain. When it aired he was still only twenty-two, and he was already amassing enough credits for his parents to understand that he'd been right about wanting to act, even when he didn't know what it meant.

As a schoolboy, the classics had never been his strong suit, but as an actor he seemed natural in the part. Of course, being written in the early 1800s, *Le Rouge et le Noir* (as it was originally titled in France) gave Sorel his comeuppance at the end, in part because he used others, but also because he was a young man from the provinces trying to climb into Society. It was social comment, after a fashion, faithfully reproduced in the series.

While Ewan understood that, it didn't bother him at all. He was resolutely apolitical, certainly when it came to acting. He was simply being someone else for a while, someone who wasn't Ewan McGregor.

Like the Irish, with whom they share common roots, the Scots have a fairly radical political tradition, and reasonably enough. During the Clearances of the 1700s, thousands of Highland families were dispossessed by absentee English landlords.

They were forced to move to the cities, which were growing at the beginning of the Industrial Revolution, or try their luck in America or Canada. It created a lingering bitterness toward the English, which the devolution of the 1990s· has barely begun to sate.

But not for Ewan. The history of Scotland had been drummed into him at school, but it didn't apply to him in the way it did to many others. His identity was himself first, an actor second, and a Scotsman third. He rarely even drank Scotch, for that matter, preferring beer whenever possible—and that meant at least a few pints every night.

Work came before any pleasure, though. With a job to do, a part to play, Ewan was focused, and the lengthy filming of *Scarlet and Black* had made him sharper than ever. He'd learned a lot at the Guildhall, but every day since on sets for films and television had been an education. Already he was developing his own style. Nothing as obvious as, say, an American movie star, who simply seemed to be himself in different costumes. But, as he pointed out, ''That's the difference between a star and an actor, I suppose. I like to think I'm an actor.''

At this stage he was definitely that. The series put his name around, and he'd done sterling work, managing to look earnest, and even angelic, on the small screen. But he was just one among many in an emerging Britpack of actors and actresses.

The previous generation, the Kenneth Branaghs and the Emma Thompsons, had fully hit their stride by 1993, and the wake they left quickly filled with young talent. For the moment, Ewan's was just another voice in the crowd, someone who'd got lucky for a while and snagged a lead role and made the best of it. But he hadn't been immediately earmarked for stardom.

What he had done was to make real strides in his first year as a professional, and even found the time to act in a short independent movie called *Family Style*, where he played Jimmy.

Filming *Scarlet and Black* in France had also given Ewan a benefit he hadn't expected, besides the chance to practice his craft and travel for free. While he was there he met a woman, Eve (pronounced "Ev") Mavourakis, who was working as a designer on the production. Ewan's French left a lot to be desired—at Morrisons it hadn't been among his better subjects—but luckily Eve could communicate well enough in English.

Love was something that hadn't been on Ewan's agenda; the only thing he'd been thinking about was his career and what he'd be doing when this was over. But love wasn't about to be denied by anything. They didn't slip away and get married, but both knew that there was enough there to continue the relationship, and the flights from London's Heathrow airport to Paris's Orly airport only took 45 minutes.

He could feel things beginning to happen, like a tide swelling. Even if he didn't have anything immediately lined up—which could have been a cause for panic in and of itself—he felt that his time was close. Maybe being in love gave him confidence, or maybe he was buoyed by having held a lead in a prestigious BCC drama.

Things looked even better when he was cast in the BBC drama, *Doggin' Around*, working with actors like Elliott Gould and Geraldine James. This seemed like a definite rung up the ladder, but the part of Tom Clayton in the televised play didn't lead to anything more.

It was back to the endless round of auditions, which were exhausting beasts, but now he had the resume and some recognition, which was something of an advantage. And his life was about to change.

Four

The team of Andrew MacDonald, Danny Boyle, and John Hodge had met by accident. MacDonald was Scottish, very middle-class, born in Glasgow but educated at boarding school in the countryside of Perthshire. Films had always been his passion—he'd made his first at school, working on Super 8 stock, inspired by *Chariots of Fire*, which was being filmed nearby. After moving to London, he began working on films, becoming a location manager, and then eventually a producer.

Along the way he did a little directing, and it was because of that that he met Hodge, whose sister, Grace, was a sound editor on a short MacDonald was directing. She suggested MacDonald and Hodge (a fellow Scot who was a medical doctor in Edinburgh with screenwriting aspirations) team up.

"So we met [in 1991]," MacDonald said, "and [Hodge] had the idea for *Shallow Grave* and started writing it and we worked on it for about fifteen months. Then we took it to Channel Four and they asked about who was going to direct it."

The pair knew they wanted someone who, like themselves, was hungry and largely unknown, but who still had the experience to do the job.

Enter Danny Boyle, originally from Manchester

in England. He had experience, having, among other things, recently directed a piece called *Mr. Wroe's Virgins*. Moreover, he was of an age with the others.

"I did admire [*Mr. Wroe's Virgins*]," said Mac-Donald, "but that wasn't what was important. We got on with Danny. He understood what we were trying to do with [our] film."

"Andrew was looking for someone who was willing to work collaboratively," Boyle recollected. "He didn't want someone with a huge track record, like a Stephen Frears or a Terry Gilliam, who was going to take over the script." He read Hodge's screenplay, and told the others, "I see this as *Blood Simple* [the 1985 Coen Brothers' film] comes to Britain." That was enough to win him the spot.

Having established the trio, and been given the budget (approximately $1.5 million), they laid the groundwork. It was a case, as MacDonald noted, of "fitting the esthetic around the budget by working with the writer and director who understood it."

The notion of filming in Scotland was something that came quite naturally, given that two of the three were from there. With the upwardly mobile characters of *Shallow Grave*, the more middle-class Edinburgh seemed a logical choice over Glasgow.

MacDonald, Hodge, and Boyle were lucky, in a way. The entire British film industry had been given a boost by the phenomenal international success of *Four Weddings and a Funeral*, which had also been funded by Channel Four. That had made it easier for domestic films to be financed and made, and for the cottage industry of filmmaking in Britain to be taken more seriously everywhere else in the world. Since then, directors like Mike Leigh and Ken

Loach had gone from national cult heroes to minor global names. Things were moving, and in the wake were opportunities for people like the troika.

Now, though, they needed actors. Ewan, though experienced and a Scot who wouldn't have to fake the accent, wasn't at all a shoo-in for the film. Like all the other actors, he had to audition.

"It was just an audition," Boyle explained. "We try to keep people and build up a pool."

"We met in a casting, like any other job," Ewan continued. "I was hauled in amongst hundreds of others and then got the job through the normal casting procedure."

At the time none of them realized how fortuitous a combination it would be for everyone concerned. Along with Kerry Fox (*An Angel at My Table, The Last Days of Chez Nous*) and Christopher Eccleston (probably best known to American audiences for his portrayal of Detective Inspector Bilborough on the British television series *Cracker*, aired on A&E), Ewan was picked to play one of the leads in *Shallow Grave*, as Alex Law, a yuppie journalist.

At the time, it was nothing more than another job, and one that wasn't especially luxurious. Wonderful as it would be to go back to Scotland as an actor, the money was nothing special, and the budget constraints meant that the shoot would have to be very quick and intense. To add to the roommate idea of the plot, the three leading actors and director Boyle shared a four-bedroom apartment in Glasgow during the filming.

That was helped by the fact that very few sets— and in particular, few costly exterior shots—were required. Almost everything revolved around the apartment that was shared by Alex, David (Eccleston), and Juliet (Fox).

It was a dream apartment, a huge place at the top of a lovely old building. The rooms were massive and airy, and all beautifully furnished, trendy and slightly offbeat, without being wild. The decor was straight out of a magazine.

All three were young and well-to-do. Alex, the most gregarious, was a journalist; Juliet, whose personality seemed to occupy the middle ground, was a doctor; and the reserved, less voluble David was a chartered accountant. They were looking for a new roommate, but they were very, very, picky, rejecting most people out of hand, and subjecting others to a barrage of basically nonsensical questions.

Until Hugo (Keith Allen). He appeared when Juliet was home, and applied for the room. He had style of a sort, attitude, and they'd tired of the application procedure. He was in.

He moved in quietly, and remained very quiet. Too quiet. After a couple of days of absolute silence from him, the others began to worry, and broke down the door to his room.

Hugo was no more; he was naked and dead on the bed, the victim of a drug overdose. As Juliet prepared to call the police, Alex rummaged around in the room (to David's disapproval), and pulled a suitcase out from under the bed. It was heavy, but when he opened it, he found it was filled to bursting point with money.

And that was where things started to go terribly, terribly wrong.

Straitlaced David was all in favor of turning everything—the body, the money, the personal effects—over to the authorities. Juliet was wavering. Alex wanted to dispose of the body and keep the cash.

Soon Juliet came over to Alex's side, and finally David was persuaded. The temptation of all that money was too much for them. But they were going to do it right. Hugo would be buried in the woods, his hands and feet removed, and his teeth knocked out. In other words, he'd be totally unidentifiable.

David drew the short straw for the gruesome work, and it unhinged him. After completing the task, he withdrew to the attic, where he'd hidden the money for safekeeping, sleeping up there on a futon, only appearing when the others weren't around. He told his employer his mother was sick and that he might be gone for some time. He was coming off the rails.

The other two were worried, partly about him, but mostly about the money. And well they might have been. Two gangsters were leaving bodies in their wake to try and find Hugo and the stash.

Even though there seemed to be no connection between Hugo and the roommates, the bad guys eventually caught up to them. By that point Juliet and Alex seemed to be on one side, and the paranoid David on the other. He was in his attic when the gangsters burst in, tied up the pair, and quickly got the information from Alex that the money was in the attic.

What they hadn't expected was to find another person up there. A changed, deadly person. David killed one gangster, then the other, and dropped their bodies down. Two more to dispose of, and he did it methodically this time.

At the apartment, there was a change in allegiances. Juliet turned to David, and began sleeping with him, leaving Alex as the outsider.

By now the police had discovered the bodies, and Alex found himself assigned to the story, something he really didn't need, especially when the police arrived at the apartment to ask questions. But the roommates all said they'd never seen Hugo or the gangsters, and there was absolutely no evidence to connect them.

The pressure was intensifying, and Alex was ready to crack. He'd even taken the phone into his room to call the police inspector, when he heard David moving around upstairs, lowering the suitcase on a rope. But Juliet had heard, too, and she wasn't going to let the money leave without her, especially as she'd secretly bought a ticket to Rio.

It all ended in violence. David pushed Alex to the kitchen floor, and literally pinned him there, with a knife. Picking up another blade, to finish him off, he was stabbed through the neck by Juliet.

Then she used her shoe to hammer the knife all the way through Alex's chest—leaving him to die while she vanished with the loot.

Except Alex didn't die, and was still quite alive when the police arrived, if somewhat the worse for wear. In the game of cross, double-cross, and triple-cross, he'd turned out to be the winner. The suitcase Juliet was dragging no longer contained the money, but cut-up newspaper—Alex's story on the three bodies. The money was safely hidden under the floorboards in the kitchen.

It was the blackest of black comedies, a tale of the way friendship could be overcome by temptation, and a lesson in how not to deviate from the straight and narrow.

Although it had been completed on a startlingly low budget, it had the look and quality of a much more expensive picture, largely because of the acting, which maintained a very high standard throughout. The three separate personalities of the roommates played off and against each other subtly. There were moments of high comedy, and high drama. And without ever saying as much, it kept asking a question of the audience—how would *you* react in a situation like this?

In Britain it proved to be remarkably successful, both critically and commercially. It took in $7.5 million at the box office, the biggest domestic film of the year, exceeding everyone's expectations, and making it a very viable candidate for export. Its success was something of a surprise, enough to make people sit up and take notice—not so much of its stars, but of the team behind it.

"There was a real atmosphere of, 'Who are these people?'" said director Boyle.

"You must understand, British audiences had lost faith with British filmmakers, and they would often go out of their way not to see British films," pointed out David Aukin of Channel Four. "What Danny, John, and Andrew did was bring excitement back."

It was an ambitious movie, for all its lack of financing, one that didn't play to the obvious, but that had been the intention of MacDonald, Hodge, and Boyle all along.

"We felt that filmmaking in Britain was totally lacking in ambition," Hodge said. "And we were never interested in making a well-regarded art film.''

''The films I like are not difficult-to-understand European art movies,'' MacDonald added. ''But I find equally painful stuff like *Twister* and *Jurassic Park II*.''

Shallow Grave owed a debt to Hitchcock; that much was obvious. But it also very much had its own identity, a very Scottish sensibility under the veneer.

What would other countries make of it, though? The dark, close-to-the-bone humor that underlay the entire story was something the British could appreciate. Elsewhere, however, people preferred things a little more obvious. In America the film grossed a disappointing $2.1 million, in spite of extensive advertising, and both Boyle and Ewan publicizing it.

But then again, although the Coen Brothers had made an early critical reputation in the U.S., *Blood Simple* hadn't exactly startled the box office, either.

The comparison with the Coens did come up in reviews (*People* felt that *Shallow Grave* recalled their ''early, skewed work''), but so did Hitchcock, although Boyle was, obviously, not as good as the master. As Lisa Schwarzbaum noted in *Entertainment Weekly*, ''Hitchcock would have limned the human condition in his characters' flaws.'' *Rolling Stone*, at least, conceded that ''the actors have a wicked ball showing their characters turn rabid,'' although the person most consistently singled out for her performance was Kerry Fox, with Ewan highlighted for his ''acid wit.''

One thing the reviewers were careful to do was warn their readers about this film. ''It begins and continues for a while as a British breeze,'' wrote Stanley Kaufmann in *New Republic*. ''Then, touch by touch . . . it becomes a different film.'' *Playboy* was much more specific. It admitted the film was ''funny at times,'' but stressed ''it's not for viewers who quail at severed limbs or at the sight of some poor fool nailed to the floor.''

The American critics all seemed to have reservations about the film, however, perhaps best summed up by *Entertainment Weekly*, which found that ''the shallowness of style over substance takes it toll.'' It hadn't been made or tailored for American audiences, however; it was a very *British* black comedy, some of which the Americans simply couldn't understand because of the cultural gap. Only *Rolling Stone* came close to a full appreciation, calling it ''a hypnotic blend of mirth and malice.'' The best *Entertainment Weekly* could manage was a comparison, of sorts, to the Oscar-winning light comedy *Forrest Gump* (1994)—which did neither movie any favors. *New Republic* took its dissection too far, wondering how three intelligent characters couldn't have been aware ''of the invisible strings'' attached to the money. Obviously, the point was missed. When it came to the money, they stopped thinking rationally. And Joanne Kaufman, in *People*, completely hedged her bets. The film, she believed, was ''too stylish and too clever by half.'' At the same time, it had ''some devilishly funny moments, and the actors make the most of every macabre one.''

It was always unlikely that America would appreciate *Shallow Grave* the way the British had. It merely underlined the differences between the countries that were actually far greater than the similarities.

By the time *Shallow Grave* actually appeared in theaters, Ewan had completed three more projects.

"*Shallow Grave* was my first movie," Ewan said. "Danny and Andrew and John are working on it for the next year, year and a half, during which time I've made three movies or so."

In actual fact, it was two television appearances and a movie. The important thing was that Ewan was working consistently. As he pointed out, from a young age he was driven, so not working frustrated him. His life had come to center around two things—work and Eve.

They were still together, still going strong, and getting closer. Marriage looked very likely; the main question was when, because Ewan was so busy.

Right after *Shallow Grave* he'd taken on a guest appearance in *Kavanagh, QC*, the series John Thaw made after *Inspector Morse* finished. Thaw played a barrister, and in the 1995 episode *Nothing But the Truth*, Ewan was David Armstrong, his client.

Immediately following that came another television guest shot, this time, strangely, in the horror anthology series *Tales From the Crypt*. Many actors of greater and lesser fame had passed through its ranks, including a then-unknown Brad Pitt in 1990, so Ewan was in good company when he played Ford in an episode called *The Cold War*.

It certainly didn't bother him to move from TV to film and back again. In fact, that was exactly the freedom he enjoyed, although he showed no real inclination for stage performance (and mostly still doesn't, though in large part that's because of his schedule: In the time it would take to rehearse and stage a play, Ewan could make two films at his present rate).

Unlike the stage, which would involve repeating the same lines night after night and becoming a character for eight performances a week, film and television offered what was essentially a quick in-and-out. It was repetition of a different kind, one that seemed to suit him well.

If Ewan in a horror series seemed unlikely—and why should it? It was just another job—then he moved next to the bizarre, a surfing comedy (with drugs), filmed in England, wearing a goatee and a wetsuit.

England does, in fact, have a part of its coastline that's celebrated among native surfers. The coast of Cornwall, in the southwest of the country, will never be a threat to California, Hawaii, or Australia, but people do go there specifically to ride the waves.

And that was the setting for the British surf movie, *Bluejuice*, about as odd a concept as anyone had come up with, but one which received financing. Ewan was cast as Dean Raymond, one of the surfing group who spent their summers hoping for the perfect wave rolling in from the Atlantic. Along with him were Sean Pertwee (the son of Jon Pertwee, known to PBS viewers as one of the incarnations of Dr. Who) as JC, and Catherine Zeta Jones (who'd become a big star in England through her appearance in the television series *The Darling Buds of May*) as Chloe.

"I had a great time, filming in Cornwall for ten weeks," he'd recall. "I've never partied so much in my life."

There was one incident in particular that would remain with him. One Tuesday evening Ewan and one of the other actors were drinking in the living room of the apartment that they'd rented for the duration of the shoot. It didn't seem as if the session had lasted too long, all drink and talk, when their driver arrived. Ewan assumed he'd come to join them for a beer, but that wasn't the case. They'd been up all night; now it was Wednesday morning, and the driver was there to take them to work.

Badly hungover, Ewan kept his sunglasses on and groped his way through the day's filming.

"It really doesn't make you feel very clever. Your acting is absolutely [terrible]."

However, in the mess that was *Bluejuice*, it was really difficult to tell. According to Ewan, the film, which never saw release outside Britain, was "a bit muddled in the middle, it's just a shame, it's not very good."

Pertwee and Zeta Jones were the stars, playing JC and Chloe. JC had made his reputation as a surfer by completing the treacherous "Boneyard" run, and Chloe ran the Aquashack, a small cafe at the beach. By now JC, approaching thirty, had given up surfing, and had purchased tickets for a round-the-world trip for himself and Chloe.

She, however, wanted to use the money to purchase the cafe. The difficulties between the pair continued when some old friends appeared—Josh (Steven Mackintosh), who loved the music known as Northern Soul, but was making his money by producing records that cashed in on the techno craze, Dean (Ewan), a drug dealer and wannabe tabloid journalist, and Terry, whom they'd brought down for a last fling before his marriage.

Dean, beaten up for selling bad drugs, begged JC to surf the Boneyard with him, since the story would get him the newspaper job he craved. Reluctantly, JC agreed. To appease Chloe, he sold his travel tickets, allowing her the money to bid for the cafe at auction, then finally refused to try surfing again. Dean did attempt the Boneyard, but had a mishap, and JC had to swim and save him. In the end, the surfing crew got together and built a new cafe for Chloe.

It wasn't the best and brightest thing ever to come out of Britain, but at least Ewan fared well. Ben Thompson wrote in *Seen and Heard* that "the film's best acting comes from . . . Ewan McGregor and Steven Mackintosh."

It was work, though, and his name was starting to become known, largely because of his work in *Shallow Grave*. What he wanted was something as meaty and challenging as Alex Law, without having to repeat the same role. His wish was about to be granted.

Five

Even before *Shallow Grave* was released in Britain, Hollywood had taken note of it. Not so much of the film itself, but of the three people who'd put it together. Boyle was offered what was to him the astronomical sum of $850,000 to direct *Alien: Resurrection*, which he turned down, and MacDonald, Hodge, and Boyle together received an offer of $250,000 from Scott Rudin, who'd been the producer behind *Sabrina* and *The Firm*, to film any project they wanted. Tempting as it sounded, MacDonald dismissed it: "... the offer was ridiculous. I mean, we haven't even met the guy."

Besides, they already had plans for their next project, a movie version of Irvine Welsh's 1993 novel, *Trainspotting*, which had caused a sensation in Britain on its publication.

The first step was acquiring the rights, which, it transpired, had already been sold to Noel Gay—the production company behind television's *Red Dwarf*. Nonetheless, Hodge wrote a first draft of the script.

"We decided to make up a few scenes," he explained, "but I can justify them all by the fact that they're all taken in some way from the novel. For example, there's a shoplifting scene that doesn't actually happen in the book. But there are loads of references to it and it's a very visual thing, so it seemed right.''

Once again, MacDonald approached Channel Four to finance the film. They were adamant that they wouldn't give a penny until the rights were all cleared.

That happened in March 1995, and Channel Four immediately committed $2.25 million. It was hardly a fortune, especially considering the success of *Shallow Grave*, which had been released in the U.K. three months before.

Boyle didn't want much money, though—an unusual note for any director.

''You can get carried away with people offering you money and end up making a film that's out of proportion with your kind of audience,'' he explained. ''But, on the other hand, we couldn't make it for [$1.5 million], so it's gone up.''

With the backing, the rights, and the screenplay, real work could begin—the whole process of pre-production. The art department was busy, locations were being sought, and the budget finalized. *Trainspotting*, it was decided, would need the relative luxury of a seven-week shoot.

And then there was casting. For Boyle and Mac-Donald, there was only one person to play the lead character, Mark Renton, and that was Ewan.

''Ewan McGregor was earmarked for the Renton role from the beginning,'' Boyle said. He was actually asked to consider it while in America, publicizing the release of *Shallow Grave*. After reading the script, ''I thought, this part is like a million birthday presents rolled into one.'' The character of Renton appealed to a certain aspect of Ewan's personality. "I liked his courage and intelligence. There's something exciting about someone that nihilistic." Hodge, though, had his reservations about the casting, as Ewan discovered later.

"John didn't think I was right to play *Trainspotting*. I only found this out recently . . . It's never been the case that I'm in the next one, not before casting."

Hodge was overruled. But there was one condition attached to the role—Ewan had to lose 28 pounds, to look more like a junkie, and he had to shave his head.

"That was just something that had to be done," Ewan said. "Renton was living a life on heroin, so he wasn't going to be a beefcake."

Even losing the weight, so often a torment for people, came easily to him.

"I stopped drinking beer and I drank wine and lots of gin instead, and the weight falls off. My wife [Ewan and Eve weren't yet married] is far more knowledgeable about nutrition than I am, and she was brilliant. She kind of told me what to eat and what not to eat. I ate four times a day but I had smaller portions . . . I didn't eat anything with any fat in it. And I didn't have any butter and I stopped taking milk in tea and coffee, not that that's going to do any good, but I did it anyway."

Now they needed the other principals, and the two they were eyeing were Ewen Bremner (Spud) and Bobby Carlyle (Begbie). Bremner was more than familiar with the plot, since he was currently playing Renton in a stage version of *Trainspotting* in London. Boyle wondered whether Bremner would be happy with the lesser role of Spud, but they both signed on without any qualms.

Jonny Lee Miller auditioned and proved to be the ideal Sick Boy. Kelly Macdonald (Diane) picked up one of the flyers circulated around Glasgow by Boyle, asking people to audition. In fact, she almost didn't try.

". . . [I]t was all these lovely girls with long locks, like models. We also had to give photographs. I had mine done in a booth half an hour before I went. They were awful. For the first round we just had to sit in front of Danny for a couple of minutes."

Nonetheless, she impressed Boyle enough to win the part.

"I knew straight away before she even sat down and opened her mouth that she was the one," Boyle observed. "There were a couple of other possibles, but you could just tell. And if you get that instinct, you know you're right."

Part of the pre-production process for the actors, and Ewan in particular, was research. He'd read the book, obviously, and came into it with a head start of sorts, already being Scottish and familiar in his bones with the attitudes of the characters. But he knew nothing about drugs.

"No, no, not at all," he replied when asked about them. "Booze, lots of booze, but that was it. I wasn't involved in the rave scene when it kicked off in the eighties. I can't remember where I was, but I wasn't there! I've never been in a drugs scene at all. . . ."

In fact, in the backwater of Crieff drugs simply hadn't been available—or a young, naive Ewan hadn't known where to look for them.

"We didn't really do any drugs because there weren't any to be had. I missed the whole rave scene and the E[cstasy] culture in the late eighties. It's quite sad. They really got the wrong guy for the job: Ewan 'Mr. Nae [No] Drugs' McGregor."

Nonetheless, until he flew from London to Glasgow to begin his research in earnest, he admitted that he did feel a slight glamor about the heroin lifestyle. But heroin chic soon gave way to heroin horror.

"I read books on crack and heroin," Ewan recalled. "Then I went up to Glasgow and met people from the Carlton Athletic Club, which is an organization of recovering heroin addicts who don't use methadone to come off [the drug]; they just come off day by day. They also play a lot of soccer."

Quite a few of those soccer games, it seemed, were played against the *Trainspotting* cast, "and they cuffed us every time. You couldn't believe they were recovering addicts 'cause they were running circles around us and we were all coughing up our last twenty cigarettes."

Being around the recovering addicts removed any final traces of glamor about drugs from his mind.

"I'm not as judgmental about drug addicts as I used to be," he added. "I know more about their suffering, their pain and their need for help."

One thing the actors had to learn was the mechanics of injecting heroin.

". . . [W]e did 'cookery' classes at Carlton. It was six actors sitting around a table with little bits of glucose powder. I always imagined that cooking a shot was ritualized, and you had to be very precise with it, but Eamon [Dohery], our drugs adviser, said, 'No, it's not a ritual—it's a pain in the arse until you get it into your arm.' It's weird how mundane it all was.''

And it was a real lesson in reality for Ewan.

"Once I started working on the film, I realized there is no romantic aspect to being a heroin addict at all. Listening to these guys' experiences, the point of despair most of them had reached was extraordinary.''

The scene where Renton appeared to mainline the drug into his body was actually shot with a prosthetic arm. The only real injection on film took place in a hospital, Ewan admitted, and "in that scene I'm getting an AIDS test, not shooting heroin. It is my arm, and that was quite good. After pretending to shoot up for six or seven weeks, it came as quite a relief to have a needle in my arm. I was like, 'Go on, stick it in me.' ''

Perhaps the most memorable scene in a film that had many occured when Renton disappeared into a toilet, searching for the opium suppositories which would see him through the first stages of cold turkey. The toilet was dirty, overflowing, unflushable.

"It was a set, of course," Ewan explained, "but it didn't really matter. It just looked disgusting, and by the end of the day I wanted to get out of there.''

It was, he noted, bleak.

"It's true to say I felt a bit sick that day. That day was like, 'Please can I get off this set, it's disgusting.' It was horrible.''

What looked like feces was actually chocolate mousse, but that hardly made it more appealing.

Like *Shallow Grave*, *Trainspotting* was set in Edinburgh, but largely filmed in Glasgow. A few of the exteriors, like Renton, Spud, and Sick Boy shoplifting at John Menzies and the ensuing chase, were filmed in Edinburgh (in that case on the famous Princes Street), with Renton being hit by a car filmed on a back street (scriptwriter Hodge played one of the pursuing security guards). That particular accident sequence, which lasted some five seconds onscreen, required two hours of filming time, and Ewan had to be hit by the vehicle 20 times—which provided lots of work for the on-set nurse.

Many of the locations really existed in Glasgow, like the Volcano club, where Renton saw Diane, or the Brewhouse in the city center, where Begbie started the bar fight.

For almost all the interiors, however, the crew took over what had once been a Will's cigarette factory, now abandoned, at 368 Alexandra Parade, in Glasgow. With 15,000 square feet of space, it offered room not only for some 30 different sets, but also the film's production offices.

Of course, there would be other location shooting, including a brief trip to the country, and three-and-a-half days in London at the end of the production.

The filming took place during May and June of 1995, a period of startlingly hot weather in Britain. Thirty-five days were budgeted for filming, working pretty much five days a week to give both cast and crew a break on the weekends. Not that the actors necessarily needed one.

"There was almost nothing difficult about [the role] because I was so prepared for it," Ewan enthused. "I had such a passion for it before we started and that stayed with me right through the shoot. It was a challenge, but that only added to it."

And that challenge, he admitted, was largely because "I had to portray something I know nothing about. But you do that as an actor all the time. The whole challenge was to channel what I had learned by hearing of people's experiences into representing the real thing."

He did a remarkably powerful job of it. Even the other actors were knocked sideways by Ewan's performance.

"Ewan McGregor does such a brilliant job in *Trainspotting*," said Jonny Lee Miller, who played Sick Boy. "I mean, he carries that film from beginning to end. You're absolutely rooted by everything he does."

It was, really, the role of a lifetime, and Ewan ate it up with relish. Everything else had been in preparation for this, it seemed.

"He lets the film happen to him and he's very crafty," was Boyle's assessment.

Ewan himself was a little more sanguine.

"I think it has a lot to do with its constituent elements. First of all, it's based on one of the best novels that I've ever read. And then, John Hodge adapted it brilliantly for film. You read the book, and you wonder how anyone could adapt it. And then Danny and Andrew are among the best directors and producers I've worked with. They and John are people who just won't be swayed from their vision. And that's because they're usually right.

"So there were all those elements, a great cast and a lot of young, passionate people involved."

The best part was working with MacDonald, Boyle, and Hodge again. There seemed to be an unspoken understanding between them. Hodge's scripts could have been tailor-made for Ewan, and

Boyle seemed to draw unusual, special performances from him.

"I just want to work with them," Ewan said
when the filming was complete. "I love it, I love
it. It'd be weird if I wasn't ever to do another film
with them."

Although he was the nominal star of *Trainspotting*, with a growing list of credits on his resume,
the filming itself wasn't going to make Ewan into
a rich man. Like the other members of the cast and
crew, he was paid $1000 a week for his talents—
about $7000 total for his participation.

Money, though, wasn't the point. Getting rich
hadn't been his reason for becoming an actor. It was
certainly far less than an American actor with similar credits would have earned, but this wasn't
America—but could *Trainspotting* even have been
made in the U.S.?

By the end of June, Ewan was finished with filming, except for a day in a studio, overdubbing dialogue that hadn't recorded well. His contribution to
the film was complete—including the shot for the
poster, of Renton soaking wet. But it wouldn't be
until February 1996—and several months later in
the U.S.—that the public would get a chance to
judge his performance.

John Hodge had done a remarkable job of adapting
Irvine Welsh's novel (Welsh appeared in the film,
playing drug dealer Mother Superior). He superimposed a structure and a plot line of sorts on a
book which, excellent as it was, rambled more
freely. Even then, there was very little linear plot
until the last half-hour.

Renton, Sick Boy, and Spud were junkies, living

in Edinburgh. Their mate, Begbie, refused to use drugs, preferring large quantities of alcohol and casual violence for his pleasure. Their other mate, Tommy, was also drug-free, entwined in a deep relationship with Lizzie.

Sick Boy, a success with women, and a walking encyclopedia of facts about Sean Connery, was a scam artist. Spud was a loser. Renton had some brains, the ability to make something of himself, if he ever chose to. He'd gone on and off heroin several times, he knew the routine, and the score.

Arrested for shoplifting, Renton and Spud found themselves in court. Spud was sent to prison, while Renton, already in a treatment program he had no intention of completing, walked free—only to overdose. Released from the hospital to his parents, they locked him in his old room at their flat to undergo a cold-turkey rehabilitation, after which he moved to London, and found a job renting apartments.

Then Begbie, on the run after an armed robbery, hid out down there, and Sick Boy arrived. But they all had to go home for Tommy's funeral. When Tommy and Lizzie had split up (indirectly because of something Renton had done), Tommy, despondent, had tried heroin—supplied by Renton—for the first time. Before anyone knew it, he was a full-fledged junkie, and dying of AIDS from shared needles. And Renton, who'd taken every risk in the book, was completely clean.

Back in Edinburgh, they'd chanced into the opportunity to sell a large quantity of heroin down South, for a tidy profit. Back in London with the drugs, setting up the meet, it was apparent that, although they were all old friends, there was little trust. In fact, the only one who seemed to have everyone's trust was Renton. Once they'd been paid, it only got worse. Still, Renton was the only trustworthy one, until he decided to make a clean break from his past, to leave Britain—taking all the money with him, dumping his friends, his family, his entire history.

It was different, surreal at times, hip without ever making heroin seem like a glamorous option, and it was certainly helped by one of the best-ever marriages of soundtrack and film, where established rock stars like Iggy Pop and Lou Reed (whose ''Perfect Day'' droned over Renton's overdose scene) rubbed shoulders with newer British acts. There was, inevitably, the Britpop of bands like Blur, Sleeper, and Pulp, but also the electronic dance music of Leftfield and Underworld (on the strength of its appearance in the film, Underworld's ''Born Slippy,'' which ran at the end as Renton walked away with the money, became a hit). The whole thing was hip, happily cynical, hilarious at some times, deadly serious at others. It was, simply, a reflection of real life, mirrored without distortion, unblinkingly.

More than anything, though, the film was Mark Renton. And Mark Renton was Ewan McGregor. More specifically, perhaps, Ewan was Renton. It was a piece of casting that worked absolutely perfectly, to the point where it seemed impossible to separate the actor and his character. Which meant it would be the part Ewan was associated with, certainly until Obi Wan. No matter how excellent his work in other films, this would be the one everyone would think of when his name was mentioned.

And, to be quite fair, he'd pulled out the performance of a lifetime.

"In a way, the movie's very much like heroin," Ewan observed. "It lets you laugh and takes you on this trip. Then it doesn't really let you have such a good time anymore."

Looked at dispassionately, Danny Boyle pointed out, there was actually very little to like about Renton, but Ewan made him appealing.

"We wanted somebody who had the quality Michael Caine's got in *Alfie* and Malcolm McDowell's got in *A Clockwork Orange*. You have a character who is actually repulsive, and yet there's a certain charm there that makes you feel deeply ambiguous about what he's doing. You're drawn to him."

Renton was cool. And so Ewan was cool, something he certainly didn't believe himself.

"No," he said. "It's like asking do you think of yourself as a sexy person. There is no answer to these questions. I don't waste my time imagining myself as these things. They are things people can think of you as."

Like it or not, as his character, Ewan was a pinup. Pushed by an aggressive advertising campaign that cost over $1 million, *Trainspotting* opened very strongly in Britain.

Film Review called it "an assault on the senses ... this devastatingly comic and tragic look at today's youth culture and their recreational habits." *Sight and Sound* pointed out that it was a film "whose tone can seem to mimic the personalities of the people it pictures. It is not a buddy-movie, nor a road-movie, nor what used to be called an underground movie." But it was superb. Writing in *Empire*, Ian Nathan gave it the highest praise: "If *Shallow Grave* was the best British film of the year, *Trainspotting* is the best British film of the decade.'' He admitted that it wasn't necessarily an easy, sit-at-home film, but that somehow didn't matter.

''Of course it's difficult, of course it's dark and dirty, violent and mean, but it is also powerfully affecting, a razor sharp, blackly comic vision of human degradation, tinged, but not let down, by a hint of optimism at the closing twist.''

And, inevitably, Ewan was covered in praise for his bravura work.

''McGregor, so good in *Shallow Grave*, matures immeasurably here,'' Nathan wrote, ''his defiant burr singing out the voiceover, his sullen, mesmerizing presence the film's heart.''

Film Review went even farther, saying, ''And if any doubt remained . . . about Ewan McGregor being our best screen actor, his beautifully rounded performance as the smart-aleck junkie Renton should scotch those doubts.''

Even as the film prepared to open, producer MacDonald didn't expect it to be huge.

''I still don't feel it will be as popular as *Shallow Grave*,'' he said. ''There's a line to cross, namely heroin, and people will feel that it's not a pleasant subject.''

What he hadn't reckoned on was the way—far beyond drugs—that the movie, as Welsh's book before it, captured the spirit of a young generation in Britain. And they flocked to the theaters to see it. It was far more popular than *Shallow Grave*, and would in fact become the British film of the year (*Sense and Sensibility*, which opened in Britain at the same time, had American financing, and was therefore not considered a *British* film per se, in spite of an entirely British cast, and a script by the very English Emma Thompson).

The next question was—what would America make of it? It would be several months before that was answered. But by the time *Trainspotting* appeared in the U.S., the ecstatic praise for both the film and Ewan's performance had filtered across the Atlantic. As a British success—the biggest thing since *Four Weddings and a Funeral*, in fact—it was highly anticipated, particularly by the young. And it didn't disappoint, at least critically.

In *Rolling Stone*, Peter Travers called it "a singular sensation, a visionary knockout spiked with insight, wild invention and outrageous wit." *Cosmopolitan* deemed it a "turbulent, hallucinatory trip" and *Playboy* summed it up as "a nose-thumbing cinematic shocker that deglamorizes drug use with frontal attacks on your senses." And, in Canada, *Maclean's* described it as "a funny, exhilarating and occasionally harrowing film about Scottish junkies."

Time pointed out that it was "a nonstop visual and aural assault . . . attention must be paid, and will be rewarded with the scabrous savor of the movie's lightning intelligence . . . a jolt of pure movie energy."

Of course, for all those who came to praise *Trainspotting*, there were a few who'd rather bury it. *People* acknowledged that the film was "often amusing and always visually nimble" but critic Leah Rozen had a problem understanding the Scottish accents and found that the "doped-up ennui eventually proves wearing," and that the film was "a little too exhilarated by its own decadent hipness." Still, that was better than John Simon, in

National Review, who seemed to want to keep the film at arm's length, as if this dose of reality was something repugnant, pointing out that "if you speak Scots, do not care about narrative logic, relish scatology, and enjoy watching heroin addicts go about their business, you will find *Trainspotting* a triumph."

His was a minority view, however.

Even its most ardent admirers admitted that the film wasn't perfect, but, as Travers explained, "there's incendiary daring in it, a willingness to go for broke that carries you over the rough spots." And a film about junkies that was slick would have simply undermined its own thesis.

While all the cast were justifiably praised (with Robert Carlyle's Begbie often singled out), it was, inevitably, Ewan who was in the spotlight, in large part because he was the main protagonist. *Rolling Stone* was awed by his "mesmerizing, maliciously funny performance," and *Time* noted that "the charm pours from Ewan McGregor's star-making turn as Renton." *Maclean's* felt that Ewan made "the movie's selfish, cynical antihero oddly likeable," and *Playboy* had him playing the role "with short-fused fervor." Even *National Review*, which was hardly falling over itself to find good things to say about the film, was forced to admit that Ewan made Renton "very nearly appealing." Perhaps the best description was in *Cosmopolitan*, of Renton, "played with wicked charm by the outwardly cool, inwardly raging Ewan McGregor."

One reservation that seemed to handicap the film, at least in the eyes of reviewers, was that it never came out and overtly stated that drugs were bad. Instead, it accepted them as a part of the characters' lives. Renton had his on-and-off smack habit; Begbie had his drinking and random violence. Drugs were a part of their make-up, and random violence was much more a typical condition in Britain—even in Edinburgh, with its high percentage of junkies—than in America. American reviewers and cinemagoers were being taken to another country, in more ways than one.

However good the reviews for both the film itself and for Ewan's work in it, it would never move beyond cult status in America, mostly because of the bleak subject matter. It certainly wasn't because of the exposure.

''[Distributor] Miramax did a brilliant job with *Trainspotting*,'' said MacDonald. But the U.S. gross—a mere $17 million—was a disappointment to the producer. ''Some syrupy Merchant Ivory film can make $30 million in the the U.S. Even *Romeo and Juliet* was able to do it—and they're all speaking in verse! *Trainspotting* should have made $35 to $40 million in the U.S. Why didn't it? I can only blame the audience.''

Whoever was to blame, those were the facts. It didn't do as well as anyone had hoped (even though it was still remarkably profitable, certainly by Hollywood standards) in America. But it remains a cult icon among a younger generation, frequently rented from video stores. And it was a prime slice of Ewan.

Although his acting might have been defined by *Trainspotting*, neither Ewan's life, nor his career, had stood still since he'd completed work on the movie.

When he was done, he had a break of a month, which he and Eve used for both a vacation and a chance to get married. In July 1995, they borrowed a villa in the French countryside, a true Van Gogh setting with banks of sunflowers surrounding the house. The wedding itself took the form of a party which stretched out for a week.

The climax was the ceremony. Surrounded by family and friends—sixty people in all—the local mayor (a farmer formally dressed in his sash of office) conducted everything in French, of which Ewan still barely understood a word. His sole contribution was to say, "Oui," when prompted. As he did so, everyone laughed, and he began to wonder if he'd opened his mouth at the wrong time.

After well over a year together, Ewan and Eve had finally tied the knot. By then, Eve was already pregnant, which was possibly another reason to marry, but hardly the main one, at least not in this day and age. Ewan might have been raised in a small, conservative town, but that didn't mean he'd kept its attitudes. He was a modern lad, and if he was marrying, it was for love. However, as he'd discover, a few people didn't react too kindly to the idea of a married Ewan.

"People are incredibly rude about it sometimes," he complained. "Like, 'What? You're married?' Strange reaction to have. Proves what people's ideas about marriage are. 'We're having a baby.' '*What?*' As if it's the end of the world. Of course, it's the start of a brilliant world."

There was barely time to recover from the party before the new husband and wife had to return to England. For Ewan it was time to get back to work.

Six

The movie industry was in a Jane Austen fever. Quite why was an interesting question. Emma Thompson's screenplay for *Sense and Sensibility* had been taking shape since 1991, and it would bring her an Academy Award in March of 1996.

Somehow, when that entered production, it started a deluge. There were television adaptations of *Pride and Prejudice* and, indeed, of *Emma*, both, unsurprisingly, with English casts and filmed to good effect in the English countryside. Even *Persuasion*, Austen's final novel, saw the light of day in a film adaptation during 1995. And to round everything off perfectly, Amy Heckerling wrote and directed *Clueless* (the movie that helped bring Alicia Silverstone to national attention), basing it loosely on one of Austen's novels—*Emma* raising its head again.

Did the world need all these adaptations? No, but there was something of a zeitgeist, as if filmmakers all across the Western hemisphere had suddenly discovered that Austen's characters, situations, and dialogue were very relevant to society of any time; satire never went out of date. And it gave them a chance to make a period drama in England, another thing that never seemed to go out of style (although

Clueless was set in contemporary California). Americans—or at least some part of America— loved those lush, *Masterpiece Theatre*-type productions, and the way the Brits did them.

Using British actors made perfect sense. Not only did they have the ability to put the words across with irony intact, but many of them had grown up reading Austen's novels in school; they were certainly familiar with them. They also happened to be very good at adapting them with a light touch, as Emma Thompson showed.

So why yet another adaptation of *Emma*? Well, this being the film industry, any bandwagon was going to be rolled until it could roll no more. A little more baffling was to have it written and directed by an American, and starring another American.

Douglas McGrath's biggest claims to fame were that he'd co-written *Bullets Over Broadway* with Woody Allen, and that he was married to Allen's associate producer, Jane Reid Martin.

"Everyone is wondering why we have chosen an American to direct and an American to star," he explained, "but the people of Woody Allen and Jane Austen are not a million miles apart." It was, perhaps, an interesting theory, if not perfectly plausible. However, McGrath certainly felt an empathy for Austen's work.

"At Princeton, where I did my degree, we read everything by Austen. I feel that many East Coast Americans, sort of the last of the Empire's colonials, are not that far removed from Austen, with their smart balls and grand lifestyles."

That worked if you were part of a social elite, with a background of money and prep school, but it was a sweeping generalization. And McGrath himself was from Texas.

It was odd enough to have *Emma* adapted by an American, but it became stranger still when McGrath cast Gwyncth Paltrow, thc daughter of actress Blythe Danner and Bruce Paltrow, as Emma Woodhouse. While she'd had several film roles, including Wendy in *Hook* and Martha in *Jefferson in Paris*, probably her greatest claim to fame was that, at the time, she was Brad Pitt's girlfriend. She'd never played anyone English. However, McGrath knew she had "a fantastic ear for accents," and when he learned she "sort of came from that East Coast Austen-ish society" he cast her.

Paltrow thought Emma "the ultimate self-deluding heroine," although "I loved and understood her immediately. Sometimes I get really fed up with her. Some days it's hard to be in the body and the mind of someone who is just so ruthless in terms of getting what she wants, even though she really believes she's helping people."

Paltrow was the only American in the cast, although there was also an Australian, Toni Collette. Collette had been the star of *Muriel's Wedding*, and was playing Harriet Smith, for whom Emma wished to find the perfect match.

The scene-stealing, such as it was, actually came from someone with connections to another Austen film. Sophie Thompson, Emma Thompson's sister, turned in a gem of a performance as the dithery spinster Miss Bates (and Phyllida Law, mother to both Sophie and Emma, played Mrs. Bates, her mother).

Ewan had been given the role of Frank Churchill, the dashing young man who comes into the society of Highbury as something of a handsome mystery, but turns out to be a cad, having deceived Emma a little. To have gone from the intensity of *Trainspotting*, followed by a wild wedding in the French countryside, to a costume drama, was something akin to culture shock. He'd already been fitted for his costumes, but nonetheless, "That was a mind-bender, having such a short gap between two such different films."

It was also his first experience with an American production. In Britain the actors weren't really treated as stars—everyone pitched in together. But America—even abroad—was obliged to treat "name" actors as stars, with all manner of conveniences, (including large trailers, where they could retire between takes), which helped ease the shock a little.

"One minute I was lying on the floor with a syringe in my arm, then I got married, then I was standing in this trailer—I'd never had a big trailer, it was quite nice—with a wig, and top hat and tails, and leather gloves on, and for a moment I thought, 'I can't go from skinhead drug addict to ha-ha-ha curly wig acting.' "

In fact, Ewan's wig wasn't in the least bit curly, and bore an uncanny resemblance to the hair he'd had in *Shallow Grave*—which had been his own. The color was the same, the length was the same. Only the style—a side part, as opposed to the center part he'd worn in real life, was different.

Although his character, Frank Churchill, didn't appear until midway through the story, Ewan was required from the beginning.

"On the first day of shooting I was riding horses and wearing a top hat, tails and gloves," he recounted. "I wondered what I was doing. Yet I enjoyed it."

The boyhood in Crieff, where he'd learned to ride, stood him in good stead for the role—or at least his first scenes, when he rescued Emma, whose carriage wheel had stuck while she was fording a stream.

Much of the filming was done at Breakspear House, a slightly dilapidated mansion in Middlesex, not too far from London, which allowed Ewan—still very much in the honeymoon phase—to commute home to Eve every night when filming was done for the day. He knew his character was unsympathetic, one of the bad guys, such as they were in Jane Austen, and admitted, "I'll probably be hated by movie audiences all over the world for being the really annoying charming guy."

It was certainly amusing to watch Ewan—so recently and so perfectly having played an Edinburgh junkie—dancing formally in breeches with Emma Woodhouse to the strains of a small orchestra, weaving in and out of couples in an elaborate dance. And it was apparent that he wasn't a perfectly natural dancer, light on his feet and elegant; he was no replacement for Fred Astaire or Gene Kelly. It was also odd to hear him sing, although he possessed a voice with good tone and clarity.

Did he do justice to Frank Churchill, whose duplicitous relationship with Emma changed the course of the story? Even he admitted he didn't. With all that had been going on beforehand, he came into the movie unprepared—something that was surprisingly unprofessional for such a workaholic. Research was one thing, but the idea of having to read an old novel reminded him too much of Morrisons Academy and homework.

"I didn't even read the novel," he admitted guiltily. "It really bored me to death. And as a result, my performance is dreadful, so there are lessons to be learned."

Emma was the tale of a young woman who thought she knew best. Having introduced her governess, Miss Taylor (Greta Scacchi) to a neighbor, Mr. Weston, and watched as they wed, Emma (Gwyneth Paltrow) believed she had a future as a matchmaker. Then, having settled on Harriet Smith (Toni Collette), the "natural" (i.e. illegitimate) daughter of an unknown man who'd been raised genteelly, as her next victim, she set about befriending her and finding her a beau. Harriet was already receiving the attentions of a local farmer, Mr. Martin, but on Emma's advice turned him down; Emma reasoned she could do much better. Her first choice was the parson, Mr. Elton. However, it turned out he was smitten with Emma, much to her dismay, and didn't care about Harriet at all. After declaring his intentions and being rebuffed, he left for Bath and returned with a bride, whom no one could stand.

Emma's good friend and brother-in-law, Mr. Knightley (Jeremy Northam) advised her not to meddle, but she was having none of it. When Mr. Weston's son, the dashing Frank Churchill (Ewan) arrived in Highbury, Emma wondered at first if she were in love with him, since he seemed to be paying a lot of attention to her. Realizing she wasn't, she attempted a match between him and Harriet.

It wasn't to be, however. What no one knew was that Churchill had been secretly engaged to another mysterious visitor, Jane Fairfax (Polly Walker), but couldn't make the news public until his rich aunt—who disapproved of Jane—died. Instead he'd been flirting with all and sundry, the kind of caddish behavior that wasn't tolerated in Highbury society.

To Emma's surprise, Harriet hadn't set her cap at Frank Churchill. The object of her affection was none other than Mr. Knightley. Once Emma discovered that, she realized what she'd never admitted to anyone, even herself—that she was in love with Knightley, and she believed he was also in love with her.

Emma was in a quandary. She didn't want to see her friend disappointed again, but she didn't want to lose Knightley, either. He took a brief trip, and on his return, he and Emma talked. He'd believed her in love with Frank Churchill, and hadn't wanted to stand in *her* way. Now that the news of Frank's engagement was out, he could state his love for Emma. And she could state hers for him.

That only left one problem—Harriet. Even that was solved, though. When Mr. Martin popped the question again, she gladly accepted. All was well that ended well.

This production of *Emma* virtually coincided with another, made for television, and starring Kate Beckinsale (*Much Ado About Nothing*) in the title role. Inevitably, the two would be compared. The teleplay was actually much truer to Jane Austen's slightly caustic novel, where Emma showed herself not to be the most likeable character.

Not that McGrath's screenplay strayed too far from the novel. However, there did seem to be a decidedly twentieth-century spin on the characters and their psychology—quite possibly because the film was very much pitched at American audiences—that never quite rang true, and his Emma was a much more agreeable person than Austen's original.

The surprise of the whole affair was Gwyneth Paltrow. Still fairly unknown as an actress, she insinuated herself very gracefully into the role, with an astonishingly perfect English accent that proved McGrath had been right to follow his instincts about her. Her only lapse, in fact, was to say "A-men," instead of the "Ah-men" that the English would naturally have said. A lot of heads turned at how good she was in the part. Even more turned at the filming when her boyfriend, Brad Pitt, came to pay her a surprise visit.

By his own estimation, Ewan hadn't been good in the part, and he was largely right. He tried to hide too much behind a big smile and a lot of bluster. Granted, he wasn't one of the leads, but he was one of the linchpins around whom the plot revolved, and his Frank Churchill didn't display as much presence—or quite as much mystery—as was really needed. Certainly, he paled a little in comparison to those around him, mostly due, as he admitted, to his lack of preparation, a mistake he'd learn from in the future.

While it didn't win any awards for its actors, this version of *Emma* did net McGrath the 1996 Writers Guild of America award for Best Adapted Screenplay, and Rachel Portman won a 1996 Academy Award for Best Original Score. (It was also nominated for Best Costume Design.)

Inevitably, however, all Austen adaptations would suffer when put next to *Sense and Sensibility*, which did an ideal job in every department.

However, both *Newsweek* and *Rolling Stone*

loved this film, ranking it on a par with both *Sense and Sensibility* and *Persuasion*. David Ansen, writing in *Newsweek*, called Gwyneth Paltrow, with her "swan-necked, elegant mischievousness . . . just one delicious flavor (albeit the most important) in McGrath's very tasty ensemble." There was praise, in fact, for the entire cast, although, he pointed out, Austen purists might quibble at some of the characterizations. He also noted that "*Emma*'s unforced charm is a remarkable achievement for a first-time writer-director . . . [McGrath] proves to be to the manner born."

Rolling Stone was even more fervent in its praise, particularly of Paltrow's bravura performance, saying that she "works such magic in *Emma* that you can almost hear the click of a career locking into high gear" (which proved to be presciently true), with a screen persona that "showcases [her] talent, wit and daring." She made the film: "It's Emma's conflicted character, made luminous by Paltrow, that intrigues audiences. The actress holds us in thrall by giving us an Emma we can love and scorn. Paltrow is hot stuff. So's the movie. It's a winner." And McGrath, reviewer Peter Travers decided, had written a script that was "faithful; fierce when it needs to be and devilishly funny . . . McGrath is a word man with an astute ear for Austen."

Fulsome words, but ones which made John Simon's criticism in *National Review* even more puzzling. After an introduction that seemed intent on showing just how erudite he could be on the subject of Jane Austen, he finally deigned to discuss the film, only to comment that "McGrath's film version, like other such adaptations, can only make [Austen's] predictability even greater," although he did concede that ''McGrath has adapted reasonably well.''

There was absolutely no mention, oddly, of Paltrow's work in the movie, but plenty of praise for most of the British cast—with one exception.

''Only Ewan McGregor,'' Simon write, ''good in a very different role in *Trainspotting*, is weak as the heartthrob Frank Churchill. Austen describes him as 'very good-looking,' and she specifies his 'height'; neither applies to the callow and stubby actor.''

Of course, Simon had been no fan of *Trainspotting*, a film he didn't seem to understand, or want to understand. And, it seemed, he wasn't that much of a fan of Ewan's, either. However, *Newsweek* stated that he ''cuts a dashing figure as the flirtatious Frank Churchill,'' and *Rolling Stone* singled him out for a part ''played with high good humor.''

While it very definitely wasn't his best work, by any means, it did all help to show his versatility. From junkie to early-nineteenth-century cad was quite a stretch, but he took it all in stride. Of course, he had played costume drama before, in *Scarlet and Black*, but that had only been seen on British television, never aired in the U.S. or released on video. If his manner seemed a little forward and modern, well, that was in keeping with the rest of the script.

In all likelihood, by the time he came to the filming, Ewan was exhausted. He was young, full of energy, and eager to work, but he'd done a lot in a very short time, and much of it had required of lot of him, mentally. There'd been *Shallow Grave*, then *Bluejuice*, after which came *The Pillow Book*, and finally *Trainspotting*. Those four projects had been completed in a year, which was a lot for any actor, particularly one who'd started out very inexperienced, with no real idea of how to pace himself.

And, as if all that weren't more than enough, he'd also gotten married, and learned he was going to become a father. Everything was good, but perhaps there were just too many good things in too short a time.

The roles had all been very different, which only stretched him further. While he'd never followed the Method and lived his characters, so much change compressed into a short space can only have added to the psychological toll on him.

At the same time, he knew he was driven. He knew full well, from his uncle and others in the profession, that work rarely came steadily, and that you just didn't turn things down. That was particularly true for someone trying to make a name for himself. So he pushed forward, kept trying for parts, and took everything that was offered. He was, however, offered virtually everything he tried for, which did complicate the situation a little. But, he reasoned, he was working, getting known (although little did he suspect just *how* known he would become once *Trainspotting* reached the theaters), and making money—something he definitely needed to think about, now that he had a family to consider. And who knew what would happen in the future? The well could easily run dry, and he might be unemployed for months on end.

What directors were discovering was what Danny Boyle had already found out—Ewan had a huge presence onscreen.

"He has that thing that Jimmy Stewart, his big hero, had," Boyle said. "He's not particularly handsome in a conventional way. He could live next to you very easily. But you get him on the screen and he's got the twinkle. The camera loves him.''

Even when he wasn't at his best—as in *Emma*—that was still perfectly true. Ewan might have considered himself nothing more than an actor, but others—directors, critics, and most particularly audiences—realized there was more to him than that. He had the indefinable star quality that set him apart. The camera wanted to linger on him. The audience wanted to know what his character was going to do next; they cared. While he sought challenges as an actor, they sought Ewan.

What he saw—in a typically self-deprecating Scottish way—as a run of extraordinary luck was more than that. The parts fell into place, one after another, because he possessed what people were looking for. With him in a film it became bigger than it had been before. Not just in terms of box office, although that was definitely the case after *Trainspotting*, but in every way. And that offered him a great deal of freedom, to take on all manner of roles, to keep pushing the envelope and veer all over the place.

Just how far he'd gone already would become evident when *The Pillow Book* (which he'd completed prior to *Trainspotting*) finally saw the light of day. He was, it appeared, an actor without limits or borders. His star had risen, and every film was pushing it higher into the sky. But the next thing people saw him in would be more than a little different.

Seven

Being naked was far more worrisome for everyone else on the set than it was for me. I actually enjoyed it, the truth be told. There was something incredibly powerful about it. Usually you'd get arrested for that sort of thing, but I got paid."

In fact, Ewan seemed to positively revel in his onscreen nudity during *The Pillow Book*.

"I'm naked a lot of the time, and they don't try to frame potted plants in front of [me] like they do in most other films. It's all part of the story. . . . I've been naked in almost everything I've been in, really," he laughed. "I have it written into my contract."

Ewan had actually made *The Pillow Book* between *Shallow Grave* and *Trainspotting*, but its release took a lot longer. It was written and directed by Peter Greenaway (and funded by Channel Four, which made it three in a row for them with Ewan). Greenaway was a British director who'd made his mark with very individual, arty films, like *The Cook, the Thief, His Wife & Her Lover*, *Prospero's Books*, and *The Draughtsman's Contract*. You didn't go to see a Peter Greenaway film simply to be entertained and taken out of yourself for a couple of hours.

The Pillow Book was no exception, although it was rather different from most of Greenaway's work. Before there'd been an almost clinical coldness and precision about his work. This was much warmer, often quite erotic, and decidedly sexual.

One thing it wasn't was easy. The dialogue was in English, Japanese, Mandarin, and Cantonese, with at least one song in French. The screen had images within images, both black-and-white and color. Visually it was absolutely beautiful, stunning. It was the work of someone in love with both images and words—words of all kinds—and finding the point where the two met, Japanese calligraphy.

Nagiko (Vivian Wu) was a young Japanese girl, whose first name was the same as Sei Shonagon, the tenth-century Japanese woman who'd written *The Pillow Book*. It is now considered an erotic classic (not to mention a landmark in women's literature), but was actually far more, a meditation on life itself.

Nagiko's father (Ken Ogata) was a writer, being blackmailed into a homosexual relationship by his publisher (Yoshi Oida). Every year, on Nagiko's birthday, her father would paint her name in calligraphy on her face.

As a young woman, she was married to a rich young man, chosen for her by her father's publisher. But it was bound to end in disaster. She loved books, and had begun her own Pillow Book, in emulation of her namesake. Her husband was boorish, loving nothing more than archery. He refused to paint his wife's name on her face when her birthday came, and deliberately set fire to her Pillow Book—which burned the house down.

She left him, and moved to Hong Kong, disap-

Ewan McGregor pays a visit to his old school, Crieff Academy.

(© TSPL/CAMERA PRESS/RETNA LTD. USA)

In his old school classroom at Crieff Academy.
(© TSPL/Camera Press/Retna Ltd. USA)

At the Independent Spirit Awards in Santa Monica with wife Eve. (© STEVE GRANITZ/RETNA LTD. USA)

With Cameron Diaz at the MTV Movie Awards.
© STEVE GRANITZ/RETNA LTD. USA)

Appearing in *Emma*.
(GRAHAM WILTSHIRE/CAMERA PRESS/RETNA LTD. USA)

pearing into a warren of cheap rooming houses, and finding work in a restaurant where she could increase her knowledge of Cantonese. Eventually she went to work for a Japanese clothes designer based in Hong Kong, and became a model—a profession where she could earn lots of money.

Her fascination with calligraphy never vanished, and she took a series of lovers who were also calligraphers, who would write on her body. None of them satisfied her, however, and then she met Jerome (Ewan), an English translator. At first, nothing happened. He wrote on her body, and she didn't find his work pleasing. Then he suggested she write on his, use him like a book, an idea she initially rejected, but which stayed with her.

She experimented on other men, also writing her words on paper, which she submitted to a publisher. The were summarily rejected.

Nagiko went to visit the publisher who'd turned down her work, but never met him; she didn't need to. Sitting in a corner, she watched as the publisher—the man who'd blackmailed her father—and Jerome left his office, exchanging a kiss. Jerome, it turned out, was bisexual.

She "accidentally" met Jerome again, and seduced him. But her intention of using him for her own ends turned against her. She fell in love with him. And he, in his own way, with her.

So when Nagiko suggested using him as her canvas, then sending him to the publisher as the first part of her manuscript, he readily agreed.

The publisher was impressed, and clerks copied the words from his flesh. Instead of returning to Nagiko, he stayed with the publisher, naked and enjoying himself.

She, believing he'd abandoned her, took other men to write on and send to the publisher, one "book" or poem on each body. It wasn't until Jerome saw the fourth book that he realized how much he cared for Nagiko, and went to her apartment. She wouldn't let him in.

He met her friend, who suggested getting her sympathy by faking an overdose. He did, entering her apartment while she was gone, preparing his body for her writing. But the pills he took killed him. Heartbroken, Nagiko wrote on him, then buried him. After that she burned everything in her apartment, and returned to Japan.

It was only later she learned that the publisher had exhumed Jerome, then literally skinned him, making the flesh into his own Pillow Book.

Now she had a mission. She sent more men, with books painted on their bodies. She wanted a bargain. As originally agreed, she'd supply thirteen books, and in return the publisher would give her the Pillow Book he had made of her lover.

The books grew more bizarre, the writing hidden—The Book of Silence was written on a tongue—until the thirteenth and final book, which was, once more, all over the body. It contained the explanation, and the finale. Nagiko identified herself, and listed the publisher's crimes. It was, she wrote, time for him to die.

He accepted his fate at the hands of the messenger, and the Pillow Book was given to Nagiko, who buried it under a bonsai tree.

However, she'd become pregnant by Jerome before he died, and gave birth to his child—their child, something positive for the future.

It was a film of moods and atmospheres, one

which relied heavily on subtle lighting effects. For something that revolved so much around words, there was surprsingly little dialogue, but this was far more about the *written* word, rather than the spoken word.

Greenaway had developed a reputation as something of an iconoclast, a person who made the films he wanted to make, rather than those guaranteed to appeal to a wide audience. It was arthouse, but on this he'd definitely outdone himself visually.

Ewan had been eager to work with him, in large part because of his reputation, knowing that any role in a Greenaway film would offer him a challenge very different from *Shallow Grave*. So, when he was offered the part of Jerome, he leaped at it.

"I read for [Greenaway] in several diffcrent accents and then he said, 'Look, you're going to be totally naked, and we need to be able to shoot anything.' I said, 'That's okay.' Then he said, 'Would you simulate sex with a woman?' 'Yeah, no problem.' 'Would you simulate sex with a man?' 'Yeah, that's okay.' So either I was the only guy in London who said yes to all these questions. . . ."

Of course, he wasn't; he was simply the right guy for the job. But he was surprised at the amount of freedom and latitude Greenaway gave his actors.

"In a way, he just lets you go," Ewan observed. "He doesn't really direct you. It's up to you to determine what to come up with. There's room to work, especially since he usually shoots long takes."

And by long, Ewan definitely meant *long*. Whereas most takes last a matter of seconds, with half a minute being long, Greenaway's would last some four minutes, an incredible amount of time, and one which offered Ewan and the others plenty of opportunity to improvise. In fact, he was very much on his own when it came to the character of Jerome.

"We never had a discussion about my character, anything. The first couple of days filming was like, 'I think you come out here and chase her down the street.' That was it. And I'm like, 'Can you give me something?' And he didn't."

Ewan was still very much the novice at this point. "I wasn't sure if I was experienced enough . . . to know how to pitch a performance . . . And it turned out to be one of the freest experiences for me."

There was freedom, too, in being in Hong Kong, which was then still a British Crown Colony before being returned to China in 1997. But Ewan's location shooting was brief. Most of his work was in the studio. And for most of his interior scenes, he needed to be naked, covered with calligraphy.

"Every morning I went into this cold studio at four in the morning and lay on a bed with heaters on each side. I [lay] on the bed for two hours while they painted my front, and I often fell asleep during it. Then I had to stand up for two hours while they painted my back, which became a bit tedious."

At the same time, it was a rather sensuous experience, "a beautiful feeling. And you don't feel really naked. It's like wearing clothes."

The calligrapher, a Japanese woman, had worked with Greenaway before, on *Prospero's Books*, and was painstaking in her accuracy. A human canvas was new, and the inks had to be just right, so the lettering wouldn't run if Ewan began to sweat under the lights.

It was, perhaps, a good job that nudity didn't bother him, as he spent much of his screen time not wearing any clothes. The irony of the fact that he could be paid for spending his days naked, as opposed to arrested, wasn't lost on him. Or his family, it seemed. His parents always brought a crowd of friends to see their son's films; they were justifiably proud of him, and the career he was carving for himself. When *The Pillow Book* opened, Ewan suggested to his father that they might not want to invite all their friends to this particular movie. A few days later, Ewan received a fax from his parents. They thought the film had been beautiful (which, indeed, it was), and his father had included a joking P.S.: "I'm glad to see you've inherited one of my major assets."

It was a film that would require a lengthy time in post-production. Greenaway had started out as a painter; one of his trademarks had always been that any individual frame from his films could stand alone as a work of art, and *The Pillow Book* seemed to take this to an extreme. Simple and spare, but at the same time very lush, there were at times split screens, screens superimposed upon screens, all manner of visual effects. That was part of what made it so gorgeous. One thing Greenaway did not do was churn out product. There was usually a three- to four-year gap between his releases, but he was busy throughout that time.

The concept of calligraphy on skin, surprisingly, was Greenaway's own. Vivian Wu, who was Chinese-American (and whose credits included *The Joy Luck Club* and *The Last Emperor*) had never heard of it before, and was a little taken aback at first. To Ewan it was even more foreign, Wu revealed, most particularly the idea of writing with brushes, as opposed to pens or pencils. However, he did try it with Eve while he was filming, and was very pleased with the results.

There was no doubt that *The Pillow Book* was an art film. It was conceived to fulfill Greenaway's personal vision; what commercial success it had would, in many ways, be incidental. It was stylized, but that was understandable. Calligraphy itself was very stylized, as was Asian life, even in the free-wheeling society of Hong Kong. Traditions were observed, and there was a heightened awareness of and respect for the past. Whereas most of the West would never have heard of the original *Pillow Book*, throughout Asia it was recognized as a classic of literature.

It was probably fortunate for Ewan to work with Greenaway before Ewan had a lengthy film career behind him, and on this film in particular; both were excellent experiences for him, as he admitted, saying, "It was a beautiful film to make and I loved working with Peter Greenaway." Young, adventurous, there was plenty that Ewan was willing to try with his character, a real sense of spontaneity that summed up Jerome's feelings for Nagiko. And he was still green enough to really let himself go, whereas a more seasoned actor might have held back.

It was interesting, too, that most of his acting was visual, something that was largely at odds with most of the training Western drama students received. In everything Ewan had done—even his monologues to get into drama school—the spoken word had been the most important thing. There had been endless emphasis on putting across the inflections and the meaning of speeches and words. But with this film he found himself in very foreign territory, where the dialogue was minimal—his longest speech was perhaps four short sentences—and his body and face became the media he had to use to show Jerome. While it cut across everything he'd learned, it was an exhaustive challenge to his creative powers. And having mastered it, it would become another tool for the future, one which would end up making him far more expressive as an actor.

But constantly learning was part of being an actor, accumulating experiences and ideas that would work sometime later, in another role.

"The people you just observe are the ones you learn the most from. It should be about surprising everyone and yourself, doing a take and thinking, 'I didn't know that was going to happen!' "

And he was still new enough to the business to be thrilled by seeing his own image on the screen. "I love to see myself up there because I can't believe it's me."

The Pillow Book gave audiences and reviewers the opportunity to see *all* of him up there. The critics did tend to agree that the film was Greenaway at his most accessible. Beyond that, their views varied wildly. *Time* thought it a film where "text and texture meet so exquisitely." *Maclean's* felt it part of the "venerable tradition of male voyeurism," although writer Brian D. Johnson did accept that in this film, "Greenaway has refined his vision to create a more palatable confection," and that "the beauty of *The Pillow Book* is in the brushstrokes."

In *Entertainment Weekly*, Owen Glieberman noted that Greenaway created "a mood of entranced playfulness"—at least, for the first half of the movie. *People* agreed, stating "Greenaway provides a visual feast, then he kills your appetite." And in *National Review*, John Simon compared it to "a twelve-course dinner consumed not consecutively but simultaneously." It overloaded the eyes with its "visual opulence."

Interview took the opposite tack, feeling that not only did "style and story mesh exquisitely," but that the film showed that "cinema can reclaim language. Exactly 70 years after the advent of the talkie stilled the visual power of silent film, words and pictures meet here, in gorgeous detente."

It was a film that would never draw mass audiences; its themes made certain of that. But it did draw plenty of opinions, for its story, its style, and its acting. By the time of its release in America, it was common knowledge that Ewan would be heading up the cast of the *Star Wars* prequels, which led to a few comments about his physical appearance. However, *People* did call him "a terrific actor," and *National Review*'s John Simon, who hadn't spared many kind words for Ewan in the past, did at least refer to him as "the rising young Scottish star" and note that he was "winning as Jerome."

The Pillow Book, however, was much more about the film itself than the people acting in it; they were little more than vehicles. Even Vivian Wu got little more than a passing mention in reviews, and that was hardly complimentary, when *National Review* called her "appealing and competent . . . but finally not quite actress or sexpot enough to draw the spectator in."

The beauty was indeed in the brushstrokes, and Greenaway had done a remarkable job of blending

East and West, man and woman, eroticism and violence, the visual and the verbal, into one complete
package.

The end of the shoot for *The Pillow Book* bled
into the beginning of Ewan's research for the role
of Renton in *Trainspotting*. The crew was filming
some final scenes for *The Pillow Book* in Luxembourg, and at a railway station Ewan saw a group
of junkies.

"I didn't hang out with them," he explained. "I
just watched them from a distance. I'd never initiate
myself into the group because that would be too
embarrassing. 'Hi, I'm going to play a drug addict,
would you like to show me how to do it?' "

It typified Ewan as an actor. Apart from the fact
that he was lucky enough to be moving from one
role straight to another, his mind never stopped
working. He was—and remains—very much a
workaholic, always craving the next project, to have
his calendar booked as far in advance as possible,
and to be looking ahead. It would have been easy
in Luxembourg to have ignored the junkies on the
station, to have put Renton out of his mind until
The Pillow Book was complete, but that wasn't a
way he could work.

After *Shallow Grave* and *Bluejuice*, *The Pillow
Book* had offered him a different way of working,
and it had enriched him as an actor. When he'd
been cast, *Shallow Grave* hadn't even reached the
theaters. By the time *The Pillow Book* was released,
Ewan was a name, largely on the basis of *Trainspotting*, which meant that his performance (not to
mention his body) was to come under much closer
scrutiny. And that was fine. He'd done the best
work he could, and he was happy with it. But it

was, probably, wrong that he was going to be judged as Ewan McGregor, star, instead of Ewan McGregor, actor.

There was little he could do about that, however; it was simply the way of the world. He'd become relatively famous, and it came with the territory, and it was going to happen more and more as he became even better known. And with the amount of projects he had stacked up, he'd need to get used to seeing his name and face in print.

Forging a career in Britain was all Ewan had ever hoped to do. While America held a certain fascination for him, in the same slightly exotic, exaggerated way it did for people from most countries, he was repulsed by the Hollywood system.

However, he was an actor, and when he was offered what he considered to be a juicy role, with other strong actors, in an American film, to be shot in Los Angeles, he wasn't about to turn it down; refusing most work was anathema to him. Instead, he decided to go and beard the lion in his lair.

On the basis of his performance in *Shallow Grave*, he'd been offered a part in an American film. Director Ole Bornedal was remaking the film he'd done in his native Denmark for a U.S. audience, and he recruited Ewan for the lead.

In was too good an opportunity to miss, to see America, specifically Los Angeles, and discover if his fears about "the biz" were founded.

However, long before the movie, *Nightwatch* (initially known as *The Late Shift*), could open, there was a slew of Ewan McGregor movies ready to hit the screen, and the first of the bunch was *Brassed Off*.

Eight

B*rassed Off* was meant to be entertainment, but it wore its political heart quite openly on its sleeve. In combining entertainment and politics it made a more effective statement than any documentary could have done, giving the audience characters—albeit fictional ones—they could care about.

At its heart was the fact that, in the late 1980s, the Conservative government in Britain, under the leadership of Prime Minister Margaret Thatcher, systematically began closing most of the coal mines.

Part of this was a heavy-handed response to what had happened in 1984, when the miners had gone on strike, refusing to be coerced by government threats (although eventually they did have to give in). Part was also because the government short-sightedly believed in the future of nuclear power as a "clean" alternative to coal. The fact that many of the mines were still economically viable held no sway with a government bent on destruction.

Since the time of the Industrial Revolution in the late 1700s, the collieries had fueled the machines and the factories of British industry. Coal from the mines had been in the fireplaces, the warmth of every English home. The pits had endured disasters where countless miners had lost their lives, but they still kept on running.

The Mine Workers' Union, under the leadership of Arthur Scargill, had always been hard-headed. They became violently opposed to the policies of Thatcher, who seemed (in the opinion of many) to treat the working class of Britain as something less than human. During the late eighties and early nineties the Tories closed some 750 mines, putting more than a quarter of a million people out of work.

In England, most of the coal fields were in the North, and the mining towns tended to be small; the pit was their only industry, and had been for as long as they existed. Generations of boys grew up and followed their fathers down the mines; without moving elsewhere, it was generally the only work available.

And it was hard, dangerous work. Even in a highly mechanized age, the miners still had to work far underground, where collapsing tunnels or explosions could easily take lives. The miners were working class, laboring with their hands. They earned every penny they were paid, and it was rarely enough.

The miners had pride, though, in the mines, and the work they did. And the more musical formed brass bands, a peculiarly Northern type of music. It wasn't just the mines. Large factories would have their own bands. Often the musicianship was quite accomplished, the arrangements elaborate, and the bands would become nationally known.

''Brassed off'' was an expression from Yorkshire, the county that was home to many of the mines. It was a diluted, front-parlor version of "pissed off." The pun worked well for the film.

It was, like most things Ewan had filmed in Britain, partly funded by Channel Four, with the rest of the money coming from the American independent studio Miramax.

The filming took place in Grimethorpe, in South Yorkshire, which had been a mining town itself until its pit was closed by the government.

"[The closure] was vindictiveness," said Pete Postlethwaite, who had the leading role of Danny in the film, "because Grimethorpe had one of the strongest unions. [Margaret Thatcher] made an example out of them, that's what she did. Out of the goodness of her bitter, twisted little mind. Lovely lady."

All the actors went into the shoot knowing the political score. Postlethwaite himself was a Northerner; he understood the working class and the culture in his bones. Ewan, too, had seen similar things in Scotland. For Tara Fitzgerald, who played Gloria, the woman who gave the band the kick they needed (as well as the romantic interest for Ewan's character), it was a shock. She'd grown up in London, and never experienced the reality of a town that had been broken like this.

"I thought I was a seasoned traveler," she said. "I'd been to New York. I'd been to the Bronx. But I was shocked. I couldn't believe that this had happened."

However, it had. The one solace Grimethorpe had was its nationally famous Colliery Band— which provided the music for the film.

Ewan's tight schedule meant that he couldn't get to Grimethorpe (renamed Grimley in the film) until

the two-month shoot began. For research, Postlethwaite and Steve Tompkinson, who played his son
Phil, went up two weeks before filming began.

"We just drove around and said, 'Hello,' and
people said 'Hello' back; after that, we were accepted. Then we started going to some of the miners' pubs, listening to their stories."

At first, the locals were somewhat suspicious of
the crew and the cast, but they had good reason. A
couple of years earlier a film crew had made a documentary about the town, which was supposed to
be sympathetic, but in the end betrayed them. There
were rumors that kids had been paid to throw rocks
at windows, so the "mindless" vandalism could be
caught on film.

"We had a great responsibility," Postlethwaite
said. "We were making a film about a community
that's been ravaged already; you don't want to go
in again and ravage them with a poor, shoddy
film."

Certainly it helped that two of the main characters could actually play brass instruments. Ewan, of
course, had been a good French horn player some
ten years before, even performing on television.
While he hadn't kept up with the instrument, as
brass gave way to rock'n'roll in his soul, he could
still, he said, "tootle along with the tunes" on the
tenor horn, which was actually a source of pride to
him. And Tara Fitzgerald had had some lessons on
the flugelhorn—enough to at least try to play with
the band.

"It was so awful," she admitted. "You think
that suddenly you might find that you've got this
gift, that you may pick up this instrument and sud-

denly produce these mellifluous notes, but this horrible sound would come out every time.''

For the citizens of Grimethorpe, the fact that the actors at least tried—however good or bad the results—meant a great deal, Postlethwaite said: ''... when the local people found out that Ewan McGregor could actually play the [French horn] and that Tara Fitzgerald could play the flugelhorn and that I could actually sort of keep them in time with the wagging stick [baton]—then the community could tell we weren't there to take advantage of them again.''

While Ewan was already familiar with brass music, the others had to get used to it, which proved remarkably easy. Postlethwaite ''listened to the soundtrack over and over again. You have to play it loud. It drove the family mad. They said, 'It's either you or that brass band—one of you has got to go.' ''

Fitzgerald bought a stack of brass-band CDs in a London record store, where ''The assistant looked at me strangely and said, 'Whatever turns you on.' The thing was, I got into the music. These miners are tough but once they start playing their instruments they become different creatures. It's very moving.'' And she had close contact with the miners, as members of the Grimethorpe Colliery Band played most of the band in the film.

For Ewan it could have been just another role, something to fill the gap between *Nightwatch* and his next project, and that could have led to a repetition of his work in *Emma*—somewhat below his usual sparkling performance. But *Brassed Off* was a film he wanted to do, partly because of its subject matter—one which could stir the hearts of many in Britain—but also because of the challenges it offered. Pete Postlethwaite had finally become acknowledged as one of the great contemporary actors, able to glide easily between stage, television, and film, and Tara Fitzgerald had also acquired a strong reputation for her movie work. Working with them would be good for Ewan; they'd stretch him. He'd be part of an ensemble again, something he definitely enjoyed.

In fact, he seemed to have a slight unease about being singled out, as he had been for his work as Renton. That he was such a standout as an actor, that the camera loved him, was just one of those things. He didn't see himself as a star, but as an *actor*, one member of the cast, one cog in the wheel of a production. He could have stayed in Hollywood and done another film on the heels of *Nightwatch* which would have increased his profile. Instead, he returned to England and worked for a lot less money on something that seemed to fit him a lot better.

"It's based on a true story and it's a really brilliantly political piece of filmmaking," he said. "The politics are so strong and the music is so emotional."

And that was what was really important. As the saying went, there were no small parts, only small actors, and Ewan was definitely not a small actor. He simply wasn't interested into buying into the Tinseltown star-making machine, an attitude that was shared by the other two principals. Fitzgerald stuck to British productions, although she had her share of the international spotlight, playing Ophelia to Ralph Fiennes's Hamlet in London and New York.

"I hate sounding worthy, but I think I like the whole process," she explained. "That's why I love British movies, because you really do feel it's hands-on, that there's no money and we're never going to get it in the can. There's something brilliant about that."

And Postlethwaite, a character actor, had made a global name for himself with *In the Name of the Father* (1994). He chose his projects not to increase his visibility or star rating, but "because they were beautifully crafted, beautifully written scripts, with directors who had fantastic visions of what they've wanted to do."

And that mirrored Ewan's ambitions. Stardom was something that had been thrust upon him, and it was still sitting somewhat uncomfortably. At least for the time he was shooting in Grimethorpe, it was a mantle he could shrug off completely.

In 1992, the fictional Grimley was at a cusp in its history. As part of its closure scheme, the government wanted to close the colliery, and the miners were scheduled to vote in a few days, given the option between a "review"—whereby a study would be undertaken to see if it was economically feasible to keep the pit open—or redundancy, with a payoff that had been heavily sweetened for "a limited time," but still only amounted to some $40,000 per miner.

Those who'd spent their time working underground knew it was just a matter of time before the end, and when the pit closed, that would be the end of the Grimley Colliery Band—no more colliery, no more band. For now, however, they'd reached the national semi-finals of the brass-band competition, under the leadership of Danny (Pete Postlethwaite), a former miner who lived, ate, and breathed music. Still, some of the band were ready to quit.

At least, until Gloria Mullins (Tara Fitzgerald) came on the scene. She'd grown up in Grimley, the granddaughter of a miner and band member, and was now back "on business," and asking if she could sit in with the band, as she played flugelhorn. Auditioning with Rodriguez's *Concerto de Aranjuez*, she proved herself to be better than competent, and was accepted by Danny, if not by all the males.

One who was happy to see her was Andy Barrow (Ewan). He and Gloria had dated briefly when they were both schoolkids, and he certainly hadn't forgotten her.

Danny's son, Phil (Steve Tompkinson), was also a member of the band, with many problems. His instrument was falling apart, and with a wife and four kids to support he was too far in debt to buy another—he was even moonlighting as a clown, Mr. Chuckles, appearing at children's parties.

The band played a competition in Saddleworth, and fared badly. It was as if none of the musicians cared any more; and most of them were ready to quit. Their entire futures were in doubt, which made the band seem like nothing in comparison.

Andy and Gloria did renew their friendship, and took it one step further than it had been before. But Andy had realized why Gloria had returned to Grimley—she was a surveyor, the person who was supposed to undertake the viability study of the Grimley mine. She protested that she was on the miners' side, that she wanted the pit to remain open.

The miners voted on their review, and the results were announced on the day the band played in the semi-finals.

The band won, which meant they'd be going to London. But the miners lost, voting 4-1 to take the redundancy pay offer. As he left the coach in Grimley, Danny, who'd been trying to hide the fact that he was suffering from the miners' disease, black lung, collapsed, and was rushed to the hospital, where he was in very serious condition.

For Phil, it seemed like the end of the road. The bailiffs had taken every scrap of furniture in his house, since he couldn't keep up the payments and his wife and kids had left him. Now his father was dying.

The band, too, had reached the end of the road. It would cost $4500 to make the trip to the finals in London, and now the money simply wouldn't be there.

Word as to Gloria's real reason for coming home had leaked out, and, in the wake of the voting results, she was shunned.

There was one last thing the band could do for their leader, however. Late that night they gathered outside the hospital in their uniforms, wearing their miners' helmets, and serenaded him with "Danny Boy." It was enough to return him to consciousness. Telling him they were all leaving was a different matter, though.

Andy, depressed, wagered his horn in a game of pool, and lost. It didn't seem to matter anymore. Everyone's world had collapsed.

Then Gloria came back again, holding a check book. The account, with exactly the money the band needed, was in the name of the Grimley Colliery Band. She'd taken the money she'd been paid for her survey and given it to the band—it was dirty money; management had never had any intention of keeping the pit open. Now they—including Gloria—were going to London!

As they played a stirring version of "The William Tell Overture" in the Albert Hall, Danny, who'd escaped from his hospital bed and made the journey alone, appeared behind them. And when the band won, he was the person who had to make the acceptance speech.

To everyone's surprise, he refused the trophy (although one of the other band members would take it later), instead making an impassioned speech about the way the government was killing the mines, and the country. His point was made, and they left the stage to a standing ovation, finishing their sightseeing tour of London, where Andy and Gloria picked up their relationship again, at the Houses of Parliament, where they played "Land of Hope and Glory" on the grass. The future might be bleak, but the band, at least, were winners.

So many films promised that they would make you laugh and make you cry, but *Brassed Off* actually delivered. There was Yorkshire humor in the way the characters talked to each other, even in the darkest moments, and there were genuinely moving scenes, such as the band gathered outside the hospital, playing, or Danny's speech in the Albert Hall (some lines of which would be sampled in 1997 as the introduction to Chumbawamba's international hit single "Tubthumping"). But, even at its most sentimental, the film never became maudlin. Mark Herman's writing and direction walked a fine line between the two, and the quality of the acting made sure it never degenerated into mawkishness.

It was a film with a point to make, and to ensure American audiences understood fully on its release here in 1997, at the introduction and conclusion fake dictionary definitions were included to plainly state what the Tory party had wrought on the mining industry, and the people who worked in it. But there were industries in the U.S. that had suffered similar fates—the auto plants of Michigan, the steel mills of Pennsylvania; in fact, production lines all over the country.

Brassed Off was, if anything, a feast of underacting. The story itself meant that no one had to go over the top. These were real people, living real lives, and there was enough drama in their stories. It was something that suited Ewan perfectly, in much the same way that *Trainspotting* had. As part of the ensemble, albeit a featured player, he was simply someone working to make the film a success, rather than have a light shone on his own performance. Given the fame he'd achieved, though, it was impossible that he wouldn't be singled out. And he was excellent, even with a hint of a Scots burr under the Yorkshire vowels. His character was a bit of a loser, still naive in the ways of the world (his idea of a big date was to take Gloria to a fish and chip shop), but with a fire for life in the eyes, and a delight in things, like playing his music well. Andy took defeat hard, but there was a sense of hope for him at the end, that with Gloria's help, he would actually have a future.

The star of *Brassed Off*, such as it had one, was Pete Postlethwaite. He turned in a finely judged performance as the music-obsessed Danny, a mild-mannered, somewhat absent man, who startled everyone with his speech at the Albert Hall, not just for its content, but also its language (the film was nominated for a British Academy Award for Best Original Screenplay in 1996). More than anyone in a fine cast, he was responsible for making the film a success.

Although Joseph Cunneen wrote in the *National Catholic Reporter* that "almost anyone but Mrs. Thatcher should like *Brassed Off*," that wasn't completely the case. *People* felt that "[director] Herman piles on more drama . . . than this slight premise can handle. The movie delivers way too much doom-and-gloom-pah-pah." And, reviewing the video release of the film, *Entertainment Weekly*, after praising the acting—and Postlethwaite in particular—decided "the script is in the wrong key."

Those did seem to be the minority opinions, however. *Maclean's* noted that it moves "from quirky comedy to high-pitched emotion with great verve," and that "the Yorkshire setting feels richly authentic, as do the characters," concluding that "even if the message blares, *Brassed Off* makes a heartfelt statement about the power, the glory—and the limitations—of music as a force to change the lives of those who make it."

In *National Review*, John Simon was full of praise, calling it "a delightful film, funny and serious by turns, perhaps a shade sentimental and manipulative. But whenever things threaten to get stuck comes some wry humor or just some sharply observed reality, aromatic, succulent, sassy."

As the *National Catholic Reporter* observed, "*Brassed Off* doesn't pretend to solve the economic problems of the coal industry or the inhabitants of

Grimley, but it makes us laugh and cheer for 'our side.' ''

Inevitably, and quite justifiably, it was Postle-thwaite who was singled out for praise. *National Review* mentioned his ''special brand of basic human dignity, usually goodhumoredly unflappable. But when emotion overcomes him, he becomes shattering as he confronts all the world's cruelty and injustice with a simple bone-deep decency, an utterly selfless pathos. His final tirade, which would sound unendurable from anyone else, issues from him rendingly right.'' And *Maclean's* pointed out ''Postlethwaite's stiff-upper-lipped patriarch.'' Even *Entertainment Weekly* had to admit he was ''terrific.''

None of the critics were as generous to either Ewan or Tara Fitzgerald. *Entertainment Weekly* called Ewan's performance ''uncommonly bland,'' and Fitzgerald ''irritatingly winsome,'' with their affair ''perfunctory.'' People at least felt they made ''an unassumingly attractive couple.'' But their romance was never more than a subtext, one, *Maclean's* thought, that ''almost gets lost in the dust,'' a point seconded by the *National Catholic Reporter*, which called it ''less successful, because too predictable.'' It was left to John Simon in the *National Review*—a man who'd shown himself to be no big fan of Ewan's in the past—to salvage things by writing that Ewan and Fitzgerald had ''a wonderfully unactorish look and feel about them.''

While hardly the box-office smash that *The Full Monty* was (and, in many ways, *The Full Monty* could almost have been the sequel to *Brassed Off*), as a movie it was most definitely a success. It was one of those pieces that could only have come out of Britain, finely tuned, walking the line close to sentimentality without ever crossing over, and powered by a whole cast of fine actors. Even its occasional predictability got turned on its head.

For Ewan, though, it was time to return to some of his favorite people. ·

Nine

Given the phenomenal international success of *Trainspotting*, it was inevitable that the winning combination of director Boyle, writer Hodge, and producer MacDonald would continue to work together.

For a while, following *Trainspotting*, Hodge had actually returned to his former profession, working as a doctor in an emergency room, just to get a perspective on real life, but he hadn't stopped writing—and Boyle and MacDonald hadn't stopped reading his words.

What the trio had in mind was something completely different, as far removed from *Trainspotting* as that had been from *Shallow Grave*. This time it would even be removed from Scotland.

It was always planned that Ewan would be a part of the team on a new movie, whatever form it took. He'd been one of the guests at Hodge's wedding, serenading the happy couple at the reception with his karaoke version of Oasis's "Champagne Supernova." (A singing reception of sorts, it had also included Boyle and MacDonald duetting on Pulp's "Common People" and Hodge singing "Always On My Mind" to his new bride.)

The question was, what form would this new film

take? They'd settled on the fact that it would be a romantic comedy. In fact, Hodge had begun work on the script that would eventually become *A Life Less Ordinary* while *Shallow Grave* was still being produced, but had put it aside. Originally set in Scotland (!), it had been moved to Europe. However, since the plot required guns, it was transferred to the one country that seemed to fit the bill— America.

But it was more than weaponry that swung the pendulum in America's favor.

"The film had to be made here, though," MacDonald said, "because Britain doesn't have the same sense of space you get in America and it's difficult to make the British landscape work cinematically—and that's one reason our previous two films were composed almost entirely of interiors."

He also thought, playfully, that it would be fun to make their type of film in the U.S. Riding on the back of their remarkable success, they presented Fox and Polygram with the script and said, "If you want to do this, it'll cost $12 million and we retain creative control." With their two previous films having made excellent profits, the green light was quick in coming, and by American standards a budget of $12 million was next to nothing.

"The only reason we're in bed with Fox is because it's a huge distribution powerhouse," MacDonald explained. "We just wanted to go with a studio this time rather than an independent company. We wanted this movie to go on a thousand screens and have real studio clout behind it."

That decision caused some consternation at Miramax, which was distributing *Trainspotting*, then opening in America, but all would eventually be happily sorted out, with MacDonald and Co. signing to make *Alien Love Triangle* with Miramax. And although they weren't handling *A Life Less Ordinary*, Miramax felt certain it would boost Ewan's star quotient in America, so much so that they postponed the release of *Nightwatch* from September 1997 to April 1998, in order to capitalize on his increased visibility and popularity.

The problem, as MacDonald admitted, was that ''we really only know America through movies,'' although ''we had no interest in making a tourist film.''

At that point, Danny Boyle did the logical thing—he decided to drive across America by himself, to see the country properly. Even then, he could only begin to scratch the surface. ''It took ten days,'' he said. ''All the virgin, empty land. I mean, there was *nobody*.'' He was amazed at ''how optimistic and bighearted the people of Middle America were'' after his previous experiences visiting New York and Los Angeles, and he returned home ''with the sense that this is a very young country with huge potential.''

Of course, it seemed odd that the group would opt to make a romantic comedy—especially one set in the United States—after doing so well with films set in urban Scotland. That, however, was precisely the point.

''I think after *Trainspotting* this is probably a bigger risk,'' Ewan explained. ''It is a different comedy to the other ones.''

''The obvious challenge after *Trainspotting* was how to build on the audience that responded to that film without simply repeating ourselves," MacDonald observed.

A Life Less Ordinary was very much in the classic cinematic tradition of boy meets girl, boy loves girl, boy loses girl, boy gets girl, but with a very modern twist.

Hodge had written the male lead specifically for Ewan, which gratified him since he was happy to be working with the team again.

"I'm just never happier than when I work with Danny," Ewan enthused. "I hope to be working with them forever."

However, rumors of other actors taking the part abounded briefly, including one that had Brad Pitt replacing Ewan.

"We met him and he was a super guy," MacDonald said, "but it wouldn't have mattered who it was, it was written for Ewan."

If there was one problem with the role, it was that the character had been written as American, and Boyle had his doubts about Ewan and the accent.

"I was doing *Nightwatch* in L.A. at the time," Ewan recalled. "I arranged for them to see five or six scenes," which would give them a chance to judge his accent. He expected a quick call back—after all, they knew each other well—but "the call didn't come that night or the next day, and it was about two days later Andrew called." Ewan, of course, was understandably eager to know what they thought.

"Well, we just know you too well," was MacDonald's reply, and Ewan assumed he'd lost the role. "And then he said, 'Oh, no, we still want you to do it, but maybe you should just be Scottish.' I didn't know whether to be pissed off that my American accent wasn't up to much or to be pleased to be in it still.''

The pleasure won out, naturally.

Since the character had originally been Scottish anyway, it didn't matter *too* much.

With Ewan finally settled in place, they now needed a female lead. For her work in *The Mask*, Cameron Diaz had been an early favorite, but also under consideration were Renee Zellweger, who'd played opposite Tom Cruise in *Jerry Maguire*, and even Julia Roberts, although, Boyle admitted, ''then it would have become a $32 million movie.''

Diaz was the final choice.

''We wanted an iconic actress,'' explained Boyle. ''. . . [W]hen we met, we knew her sense of humor would work well with ours—she has a peculiarly un-American sense of humor.''

''Immediately Ewan and I just fit,'' Diaz said, which was really just as well, all things considered.

''It would have been a nightmare if we hadn't,'' Ewan admitted. ''All that romance stuff was so there, and our eyes were just twinkling away at each other. It would have been impossible to create that with someone you didn't like.'' And though he'd wondered what it would be like to play love scenes with an American, he conceded that, ''She's not in any way what you might fear from an American movie star,'' which ranked as a high compliment.

And the emphasis was on ''like''; though they played a romantic couple in the film, there was nothing like that between the pair in real life. Ewan was a happily married man with a young baby, and both Eve and Clara accompanied him on location.

* * *

Exactly where the location would be was another hurdle for the team to surmount. At first they looked at North Carolina, but, said Boyle, ''it was so rainy and misty it was like Indonesia. Then everybody kept talking about these wonderful mountains in Utah.''

And more problems were cropping up—this time with the script. Although creative control had been written into the contract, Fox still offered suggestions to Hodge about his writing.

''There was some concern about the opening scene, in which Cameron Diaz shoots her fiancé in the head. Also, someone suggested that there should be a table-tennis scene, in the wake of *Forrest Gump*, I guess.''

The first point was perhaps well made, at least for American audiences. But then, according to Boyle, ''Fox were on about that they've got to kiss every ten minutes,'' which, he finally figured out, meant more close-ups, rather than the actual meeting of lips.

Utah was visited, and approved, so now it was time to bring the full crew on board. That meant many of those who'd worked on *Trainspotting* would be returning, including cinematographer Brian Tufano, editor Masahiro Hirakubo, production designer Kave Quinn, and costume designer Rachael Flemming, the people who'd helped contribute to the very distinctive look of Boyle's last two films.

As before, art gave a strong influence to the overall plan, in this case the paintings of artist R. B. Kitaj, the photographs of Henri Cartier-Bresson, and *Dirty Windows*, a photo-essay by Mary Alpern which dealt erotically with voyeurism (". . . In fact, we include a little homage to her in the film," Boyle said).

As a location, Utah proved to be excellent. There was the beauty of the Wasatch mountain range, utilized to good visual effect, the sheer wideness of the vista, which couldn't happen in Europe, and the financial advantages of cheap non-union labor, to ease the costs of making the film.

What neither the production team nor the cast had realized was just how strongly Mormon the state was. With its specific religious tenets, including no alcohol, no tobacco, and no caffeine, the religion demanded a very strict lifestyle from its adherents, and that meant bars were fewer and farther between than in the rest of the country.

"I'm American, and it was culture shock for me," Diaz said. "But it was especially hard for those guys, with the strict no-alcohol rule in Utah. They are, after all, British."

Boyle agreed that it was "a very weird place. Utah's intensely moral and they're desperately concerned about crime, yet there's no morality about business. It's one of just two U.S. states where there's no limit on interest rates you can charge some poor widow who borrows money foolishly, so the morality doesn't extend to the economy."

Nor did the morality always extend to the production of *A Life Less Ordinary*. When it was revealed to locals that two of the characters in the film would be angels who carried guns and engaged in physical violence, it became impossible to find extras—they had to be bussed in from other states. Then there was the security guard. . . .

The man who was playing the guard at the bank Ewan's and Diaz's characters were robbing was supposed to be filmed sitting on the toilet. He refused, however, because he was wearing his "sacred Mormon underwear." Only other members of the Temple were allowed to see it, not outsiders, and definitely not millions of people in movie theaters. At first Boyle thought he was joking, but the story turned out to be completely true.

Ewan and Diaz prepared for the movie in the most obvious way, by watching some of the great old romantic comedies. Together, in the Tower Theatre in Salt Lake City, they had a special screening of the classic 1934 Frank Capra film, *It Happened One Night*, where the male and female characters attempt to outdo each other.

"Ewan and I were sitting there sneaking smokes," Diaz related.

Holly Hunter entered the picture as one of the angels because of a meeting at the Cannes Film Festival. She'd worked with the Coen brothers on *Raising Arizona* (1987), and was in France to help promote the controversial film *Crash*, an adaptation of the J. G. Ballard novel. The Coens were there with *Fargo*, and MacDonald, Boyle, and Hodge had gone to push *Trainspotting*, "so it was a gold mine in terms of strong points of view around the table," Hunter recalled. Having gotten to know the British troika, she came to mind for them because of her strong skills with characters.

Ewan himself proved not to be a big fan of Utah. "I hated it," he said bluntly. "It's a beautiful place, but the people . . ." Clara, six months old when filming began in August 1996, and Eve traveled with him. "I'd walk around with my baby and I'd be stared at because I don't dress like a Mormon . . . thank God! I'm a scruffy young guy with a baby, and they looked at me like I was Satan himself. I have this woolly hat with 'PERVERT' on the front, so I put it on [Clara] and walked around like that.''

It also annoyed him that, at twenty-six, he was asked for proof of his age when he went into a convenience store to buy cigarettes. He went so far as to call it ''the most close-minded, uptight place I've ever been,'' although time and distance would mellow his attitude to: ''I have no problem with the place, and it's a beautiful state. I would apologize to [all the residents] if I could.''

However, while he was there he certainly didn't fall in love with it. With a shoot set for fifty days, he had to grind his way through the best part of two months in the Beehive State. They filmed from Monday to Friday, giving everyone the weekend off, when Ewan and Danny Boyle would adjourn to Spankies, one of Utah's very few biker bars, to drink and play pool.

''One night, I beat Danny on the pool table. The next day he said he couldn't believe it because I was so drunk I could hardly speak and yet I was hammering the balls in one after another.''

The visual centerpiece of *A Life Less Ordinary* was the bizarre karaoke scene, where Robert (Ewan) and Celine (Diaz) went to a bar and performed a karaoke version of the fifties Bobby Darin hit, ''Beyond the Sea,'' that turned into a full song-and-dance number, with full costumes. Like *Shallow Grave*, it gave Ewan a couple of seconds on the drums to relive his youthful past with Scarlet Pride, and also the chance to dance the way he had in *Lipstick on Your Collar*, the kind of jokey self-referencing that made it all seem like family. To rehearse the scene, they made the obvious decision—perform it.

However, Boyle's idea of rehearsal was a little different from that of Ewan and Diaz. He took them to the Silver Bullet, a Salt Lake City country-and-western bar one night, and had them perform it in front of a real audience of locals. They agreed, but on one condition—that Boyle would also perform a song. And not just any song, but the Sid Vicious punk version of Frank Sinatra's "My Way."

"Danny's very shy, but he got up onstage. . . ." Diaz recounted. "And he has that naturally spiky hair. The cowboys were into it, but when we were walking to the car, which was the only non-pickup truck in the lot, I was saying, 'C'mon, hurry up.' "

Breaking their previous tradition, Boyle and company had no nudity or sex in this movie.

"The dance at the karaoke is the sex scene," Boyle explained. "This is supposed to be some kind of romance. We can't do a sex scene, because you'd have to have tissues and condoms and things. It just didn't seem right for this particular kind of film, so we thought we'll have this dance instead, which is a very old-fashioned way. That's the way they used to do it in the old days, isn't it?"

But blatant sex was hardly necessary. Some scenes were rehearsed, but never filmed.

"I've never seen anything as sexy as Cameron Diaz not wearing any trousers walking down the staircase," Ewan said. "That's about as much sex as you could want in a movie, I would have thought."

In spite of initial fears, interference from Fox was minimal as the filming proceeded. In fact, the studio, with its knowledge of American audiences, ended up offering some very good advice. As originally written, the bank robbery scene had Diaz holding a gun to the head of a seven-year-old girl. Fox said they could go ahead and do it, but American audiences—and from the beginning, the intention was to aim this film at America, even if it wasn't really an American film—would hate it. So, in the end, the girl became a teenager.

As to the question of what a Scot would be doing in America, it never even seemed to arise. As Ewan noted, "He's there because he's there."

And Boyle added, "We wanted him to play somebody lost in America, without any family. And because he's Scottish rather than British, hopefully you evoke on some subconscious level Sean Connery rather than Hugh Grant."

Whatever his character's nationality, it was quite obvious by now that Ewan was a star to other people, even if he didn't want to admit it himself.

"All the girls have been coming up to him and saying, 'Ewan McGregor, we're in love with you. You're married and have a baby, it's not fair,' " said Diaz. "And he makes acting look so easy. He doesn't beat himself up over it."

With the filming of *A Life Less Ordinary* complete, Ewan did use his star status to obtain one favor—the chance to have a role in one of his favorite television shows, *ER*. It had all been negotiated through his agent, of course, but once he was done, Ewan flew from Salt Lake City to Los Angeles for the taping.

ER, the hospital drama series, had become something of a TV phenomenon, making stars of George Clooney and Noah Wyle. Ewan's clout got him a part that was more than a cameo, but instead something sustained through the entire episode called *The Long Way Around*, which was aired in 1997.

He played Duncan, a Scotsman who was down on his luck, and reduced to robbing a convenience store with his friend. What should have been simple and quick turned into a standoff, with Nurse Hathaway (Julianna Margulies) taken hostage by Duncan. After he was shot, it was up to her to help keep him alive until an ambulance could get him to the hospital.

The show didn't rank among Ewan's finest onscreen moments, in part because of the clichéd plot and dialogue. But there was also a sense that he just no longer quite fit in TV, even though he'd begun his career there. To try and underact, he came across as barely even there.

But it was a diversion. Filming *A Life Less Ordinary* had been the main event, and working with Boyle, MacDonald, and Hodge had been a real joy for him.

"I'd be delighted to speak John Hodge's dialogue for the rest of my life," Ewan enthused. "And Danny seems to be the man who pulls the best work out of me. Their loyalty has been beyond the call of duty, but they won't let their loyalty get in the way of producing the movie they want to make."

Already, as Boyle flew back to England to begin editing *A Life Less Ordinary*, there was talk of Ewan working with the trio again, on an adaptation of *The Beach*, Alex Garland's novel about backpackers traveling from island to island in Southeast Asia, searching for a fabled paradise.

And as for the troika, they certainly wanted

Ewan back, for more than his star power. It was simply a team that worked well together.

"How many [films] has De Niro done with Scorsese?" MacDonald wondered. "Or Mastroianni with Fellini? Danny and Ewan still have a ways to go, haven't they?"

But it was just one of many things on Ewan's calendar. Everybody wanted him in their film, it seemed. The offers were coming in faster than he'd ever expected, as people saw his movies and realized just how big his talent was.

The strength of that talent and presence, and the way it continued to grow, was perfectly evident in *A Life Less Ordinary.* Diaz was Celine, the spoiled little rich girl whose sheltered life forced her to extremes, like shooting apples off people's heads. It worked well with the butler, but her fiance, a self-absorbed dentist, moved at the wrong moment, and ended up in the hospital. Her father, the head of a large corporation, determined it was about time she began to work, and appreciate the value of money.

Robert (Ewan), knew money's value down to the last penny. He was a janitor at the corporation, or he had been until he was replaced by a robot and fired. The same day, his girlfriend left him. Could his life have got any worse?

Indeed it could, and it did. Up in heaven (which looked like a police precinct with everything painted white), two angels (Holly Hunter, Delroy Lindo) were on probation. Their track record of bringing couples together hadn't been good. This new case was their last chance. If it didn't work out, they'd be left on earth. The couple was Robert and Celine. And to start the proceedings, they posed as debt collectors, repossessing all of Robert's furniture and his car, and evicting him from his apartment.

If he wasn't already, Robert was now a loser, who could go no lower. Furious, he forced his way in to see the head of the corporation, intending to use a gun to demand his job back. Unfortunately, this was when Celine was being read the riot act. After almost bungling everything, Robert escaped, with Celine as his hostage. He was flustered; she was calm and collected.

Driving out into the wilderness, Robert broke into a cabin, and tied Celine to a chair before going into town to buy groceries. On his return, she was free, sitting and reading a book. She'd been kidnapped before, and knew it would be a great way to exact financial revenge on her father.

Robert, of course, blew the ransom demand. He was too polite, too much the nice guy. Finally Celine had to do it herself, screaming on the phone.

Her father, meanwhile, had hired a pair of bounty hunters—the angels—to bring back his daughter and kill Robert.

The first attempt to collect the ransom didn't work, and Robert, true to form, ended up losing the car. At the cabin, they came under the scrutiny of a neighbor, and only satisfied his curiosity when Celine (dressed only in a sheet) said that Robert was a rock star, and they were on their honeymoon. That would come back to haunt them when they went down to the local bar, and ended up being forced to take part in the local karaoke night.

The second attempt to collect the ransom seemed to go well, except that Robert stopped to help an injured pedestrian—who turned out to be one of the angels, carrying a gun. Putting the pair in jeopardy, the angels thought, would bring them together, and the biggest jeopardy would be to kill Robert, after making him dig his own grave. To a point, they were right. Celine did rescue him, and they took off. But they didn't have the ransom money.

Instead, Celine suggested bank robbery as a career option. But when they attempted it, Robert was shot in the leg, and it was up to Celine's former fiance, the dentist, to patch him up.

After that, they split up, Celine going to live with her mother, Robert working as a janitor in a cheap bar. If the angels were ever going to get back into heaven, they had to do something.

A love poem was the answer, and it seemed to work. Celine came down to the bar. But although Robert loved her, he was too honest for his own good, denying he'd ever written it.

In desperation, the angels kidnapped her. If they couldn't bring the pair together, at least they could be rich. Robert tracked them down, and was about to free her, when her father and the butler arrived, with guns, shooting both the angels. He wanted his money.

It was back to the cabin, Celine locked in the trunk, with Robert desperately looking for the loot— which wasn't there. Finally, his time was up. But just as he was about to be shot, God sanctioned a miracle; the bullet passed through his heart, but he was alive. The angels freed Celine, and they escaped, to live happily ever after.

As a little tag, over the credits came a claymation film, of Robert and Celine escaping in a Volkswagen, with the bag of money, and ending up in Scotland, where they bought a castle. Made by Mike

Mort of Passion Pictures, it tied up all the loose ends, which, according to a test audience, had been left undone. It emphasized the fact that Robert and Celine did live happily ever after, as well as adding a very quirky ending to a very quirky film.

And quirky it definitely was, melding a very British sensibility onto a decidedly American genre. While it was a romantic comedy, a better description would have been postmodern romantic comedy, with the humor very dark indeed. There were some hilarious moments, and Ewan was awkward and appealing as Robert, the loser who wasn't really a loser, but just a genuinely nice person overtaken by circumstance, and falling deeper and deeper into a situation he didn't understand. Cameron Diaz was sassy, commanding, and sexy, exactly what Celine needed to be, and the sparks did increase between them as the movie progressed.

There was also some humorous self-referencing on the part of the filmmakers: the grave in the woods, a bag of money, and people being hit in the head with shovels all harkened back to *Shallow Grave*, while the close-up of the scalpel opening up Robert's bullet wound brought to mind a scene from *Trainspotting*.

The song-and-dance scene in the karaoke bar was bizarre, but lunatic and rough enough in its inception to work as gleeful homage to the old movies, and the desperate angels were a lovely touch.

It wasn't funny in the traditional manner, but sneaked up on the viewer, always taking the oblique angle, homing in on the blackest moment and highlighting it.

As with the other two films this group had made, it was driven by character rather than plot, depending on, and in the end succeeding, because of Ewan and Diaz. They held everything together, the hapless Robert trying to happen to life, instead of it happening to him, and Diaz, the calm, collected one, getting in way over her head. But everyone gave sterling performances. While it wasn't the unmitigated triumph of *Trainspotting* (and it would have been virtually impossible for this film to match that), it was still a victory.

Unfortunately, that wasn't the way the critics saw it. *Maclean's* seemed to sum up the general feeling when it called *A Life Less Ordinary* "not entirely disastrous, but it is a major disappointment considering the talent of those involved," and that it was "a coy, self-indulgent pastiche that is not just off-kilter but all over the map." *Variety* summed it up as "part kooky romance, part screwball comedy, part quirky fantasy and part *Roadrunner* cartoon, this is a movie that has everything except an involving storyline and characters." *Entertainment Weekly* wondered "how can a movie this bad have been created by . . . the same team that made *Trainspotting*?" before answering that "sometimes, it takes people this talented to misfire this completely." *People* dismissed it as "derailed." Only *Rolling Stone* came out in its defense, observing that "the kinks kick in soon enough to turn this piffle into a profanely funny romance," and comparing it to "the Marx Brothers and the Coen boys collaborating on a valentine spiked with mirth and malice." (*Maclean's* evoked the Coens and Frank Capra.)

The main problem seemed to be all the confusion and the clutter. Some questioned why Hunter and Lindo, as the angels, were even in the film. It was a movie the writers wanted to like, but most couldn't. It "offers some moments of fun and a few of genuine inspiration," Derek Elley wrote in *Variety*. "But the simple, and potentially affecting, coed romance lying at its heart rarely gets a chance to stand tall amid the crossfire of mismatched ideas."

There was also doubt about the pairing of Ewan and Cameron Diaz. *Maclean's* decided that she "seems out of her depth as the bitchy smart blond," and noted that "the movie's runaway whimsy fails to camouflage a lack of chemistry between the two leads, who are extremely cute but oddly mismatched." *Entertainment Weekly* echoed that view, saying "she delivers her lines in the bored whine of a suburban mall queen." Again, it was left to *Rolling Stone* to call her "the real deal in screen sizzle."

And how did Ewan fare at the hands of the reviewers? This was, after all, his highest-profile part since his name had become known, and his big American lead. He emerged a little better than any other part of the film, at least. To *Entertainment Weekly*, he was "mopey and precious—a Scottish Andrew McCarthy." In *Maclean's*, Brian D. Johnson seemed to feel sympathy for Ewan, "an actor bristling with intelligence and wit, [who] seems dying to burst out of his dumb-and-dumber role as the male ingenue." And *Variety* did concede that he was "very good, with boyish appeal to spare." *Rolling Stone* thought he had "a ball playing a dim bulb."

However much the critics had wanted wanted to like it, though, most simply couldn't recommend it, hardly the kind of endorsement Boyle, Hodge, and

MacDonald were hoping to receive. America had been their great hope. After two huge successes in Britain, they were well aware that it might—in tried and true journalistic fashion—be time for the backlash against them to begin. That wasn't quite the case, however. Film magazine *Empire* fairly assessed its good and bad points, noting that it contained "scalpel-sharp direction, nicely judged performances, a believable chemistry between the leads. But," writer Caroline Westbrook continued, "crucially the spark, the sheer thrill and enthusiasm that ignited [the team's] predecessors, is noticeably absent." She did have kind words for Ewan, though, complimenting him on "doing hapless with ease to create his most sympathetic character to date." (She also called Diaz "the closest thing to luminous in the whole movie.")

Sky International was far more enthusiastic, deeming it "visually sumptuous, tightly scripted and one hundred per cent schmaltz-free. A brilliant, deranged, heart-melting, high-speed romance that'll make you feel glad to be alive and restore your faith in love." Reviewer Sophie Wilson also delighted in the way the leads were "cast against type. McGregor, usually so devilish, revels as an endearing klutzy side."

And so it didn't fare too badly at home, certainly better than the filmmakers had hoped. But it wasn't quite the success they'd aimed for.

Ewan wasn't transformed into a major star by the appearance, either, although that had never been his aim. But it did add to—and certainly not tarnish—his reputation.

Ten

Finally it was time for *Nightwatch*, the film Ewan had made in Los Angeles before *A Life Less Ordinary*, to find its way to the theaters. It wasn't released until April 1998 in an attempt to capitalize on Ewan's raised profile—an attempt that turned out to be rather fruitless.

Ewan loved acting, and he was certainly doing enough of it, but he hated the business side of the profession. In Britain he was able to get on with it and work on his craft, even if it wasn't going to make him rich. America, or more specifically Hollywood, was a different matter altogether. When money became the bottom line, rather than art, everything suffered, and there was one example he was always happy to point out—*Independence Day*. It was "an abomination," a movie that disgusted him (to the extent that he seriously believed the actors should have had their Equity cards revoked) with its poor writing, poor acting, and over-reliance on special effects, rather than people, to carry it all.

"[Movies are] such a huge industry in America—there are films made here that cost $200 million, which is a disgrace," he complained. "Think what $200 million could do in the world, and they're making a movie with it? It's sick, and anyone involved with that kind of filmmaking should be ashamed of themselves.''

Los Angeles, of course, was the epicenter of the movie business.

''I don't like it there,'' Ewan said firmly. ''The way they just talk business. It has nothing to do with making good films. The studio system in L.A. is about A-list, B-list and C-list. About money. They just make me cold and they turn out such awful [stuff].''

That didn't mean, however, that he couldn't be tempted to work in L.A., just that it wasn't going to be a big part of his life.

''If I want to do a film in Hollywood, I'll do it, but I'll come back [home].''

He lived in Britain; he was a British actor who much preferred the British system, where small, quirky productions could slip through the net and onto the screen, and a film could be made for a sum less than the gross national product of many countries.

That said, Hollywood could be seductive, even to someone as principled as Ewan. And when it came calling with a very good script, Ewan didn't simply close the door. Instead he looked very closely at what was on offer.

In this case it was a project called *Nightwatch* (or *The Late Shift*, as it was known then), which would be a very small film by American standards, with no special effects and no massive budget. The other actors already cast—Nick Nolte, Patricia Arquette, and Josh Brolin—were *actors*, not movie stars. Interestingly, it wasn't really an American film. *Nightwatch* had begun life as a Danish movie, a big hit over there, a thriller about a student who worked the night shift in a morgue while a killer was on the loose in the city. Its director had been Ole Bornedal, and Miramax had offered him the chance to come to L.A. and make an American version of the film. It was an offer that was difficult to refuse, and Bornedal didn't even try.

"I wonder if he just directed the same film again, I don't know," Ewan mused later. "He's got a great director of photography, who's Danish and also worked on the first version."

The script, and the fact that this was going to be low-key, not any kind of blockbuster, was enough to convince Ewan to sign on the dotted line. Working with good American actors also attracted him, and so, with baby Clara Mathilde just a few weeks old, Ewan packed his bags and flew to the West Coast.

It wasn't what he expected. For people in movies, L.A. is a town that revolves around the business and the deal. It's about being seen in the right places, with the right people, at the right time. In other words, it was everything he loathed. Unlike most people in films, he didn't even have a publicist. Why would he need one? He was an actor, not a celebrity. The only time he wanted to talk to the press was when he had a new film coming out.

When he met with agents in Los Angeles, they'd try to educate him in the ways of the Hollywood world, advising him to do two films for himself, and then two for "the business," which rankled sorely; that wasn't the way he wanted to work. "You do every film because you want to do good work. Because you're interested in making good movies and working with good people."

Another taste of American movie reality came when he sat in on a business meeting.

"They all talk about budgets and meetings—the last thing anybody seems to be worried about is the movie. A-lists and B-lists of actors—that's disgusting. 'We got a B-lister and a couple of C's, now we need a couple of A's.' No no no no, you don't; you need *the right person for the part.*"

It was where the British and American ideals clashed; in Britain actors weren't so obsessed by the idea of stardom, and there was less prejudice between different mediums. Actors could move back and forth between film and television, and often stage, without feeling that it made a difference in their careers; there was more freedom.

Working and staying in Tinseltown had an odd effect on Ewan. Although he'd lived in London for six years, he found himself beginning to crave the countryside. His days shifted between the soundstage and the hotel, work, eat, and sleep. The sprawling, smoggy mass that was greater Los Angeles seemed to offer very little green—no small parks, no places he could just walk and forget everything. So he began doing something he'd never expected to do—watching golf on television. He hadn't played the game since he was a teenager, but somehow its slow, lulling rhythm, and the vast green expanses of the course soothed his frazzled nerves. It was homesickness, really, and even if it was for a life he'd rejected, there was something comforting in it. When he was really missing home, he'd begin to utter London street names like a mantra, conjuring up the pictures in his mind as if he were actually there, rather than here in Hollywood.

When the film's producers wanted to reshoot

some scenes to make Ewan's character more of an action hero, he refused; that wasn't what he'd agreed, it wasn't the character as written. More than that, it wasn't him.

While he knew he didn't particularly care for Los Angeles, Hollywood wasn't sure what to make of him. He was a name, mostly thanks to the international success of *Trainspotting*, but as far as his other credits went, the executives of Hollywood looked at British movies "as we would view psychedelic Polish movies from the '50s," i.e., askance.

Some people blankly refused to believe there could even *be* any kind of film industry outside the West Coast. When Ewan met a young actress, she asked, " 'How long have you been in L.A.?' I said, 'Well, actually, I live in London.' She said, 'How does that work?' *How does that work?* She couldn't imagine that anyone could make movies outside of L.A."

The work itself, his real reason for being there, went smoothly enough, and he enjoyed working with Nolte, Arquette, and Brolin, three people who hadn't really bought into the star system, although Nolte was, in his own way, quite a big name. They'd managed to stay somewhat beneath the radar. Nolte had moved between big hits like 1982's *48 HRS.* and the more offbeat, but critically acclaimed *Lorenzo's Oil* (1992). With the exception of 1992's *Ethan Frome*, virtually all of Patricia Arquette's films had been small and quirky, but along the way she'd developed a strong reputation as an actress, possibly even bigger than her sister, Rosanna. Brolin was a young, intense character actor who'd started out young in the 1980s kids' film *The*

Goonies, and stuck around as an adult to have roles in movies like *Flirting with Disaster* and *Mimic*.

These were people who, like Ewan, valued acting for its own sake, people with whom he could be quite comfortable. It made for a good, easy working atmosphere, everyone prepared and professional. Even though, as he learned, Ewan's American accent left a lot to be desired, it didn't really matter. What was important was how convincing he was in the role.

Still, it was with real feelings of relief that he went back to London, to see Eve and Clara. The experience had been interesting, and certainly educational, but he was glad to see the last of Los Angeles as the plane took off from LAX. The cut and thrust of Hollywood, the entire way it worked, just wasn't for him. He was much happier in London, working in an environment he understood, and where the people understood him, where he could get drunk if he wanted, and no one thought anything of it, where it wasn't a big deal. He left America unimpressed.

Nightwatch was, in essence, the story of a young man unwittingly drawn into something much bigger than himself. Martin Bells (Ewan) was in his final year of law school. He lived with his girlfriend, Katherine (Patricia Arquette), an actress, and they spent their free time with Martin's friend James (Josh Brolin) and his girlfriend.

To help pay his bills, Martin had just found a job as the night security guard at the morgue. A serial killer was on the loose, murdering prostitutes and cutting out their eyes.

James, in a fit of post-adolescent angst, decided

he could feel nothing, that emotionally he was completely numb, and wanted to push himself to extremes, in order to try and feel anything at all. He'd been with a prostitute, and he provoked a fight in a bar—getting himself beaten up. He challenged Martin to spend time with Joyce, the hooker he'd met, explaining that when he'd picked her up, he'd told her *his* name was Martin.

He also sneaked into the morgue when Martin was working, and set off the alarm, pretending to be a corpse who'd come back to life.

When a new victim of the killer was brought in, Martin met the cop in charge of the case, Inspector Cray (Nick Nolte), a gruff cop full of theories and experience.

Martin met Joyce in a restaurant. To keep up James's pretense, Martin was now known to her as James. She had, it transpired, been a friend of the killer's most recent victim.

Soon Martin began getting calls from Joyce—calls that Katherine took, and it was fracturing their relationship. At work, things also got freaky. Someone moved a corpse, then put it back, making Martin look like a fool when he raised the alarm. Then someone had sex with the corpse, and Martin was the obvious suspect.

His life was taking an odd turn—he was being set up, but he had no idea why, or by whom. Martin confided in Cray, who said he believed him.

Finally, there was a call from Joyce, asking him to come to her apartment. He never received it; instead Katherine went. She found Joyce dead on the bed, and the killer—whom she didn't see—in the bathroom. She managed to sneak out before Cray (revealed as the murderer) emerged, using Joyce's blood to write "MARTI—" on the sheet.

Cray's assistant came to Martin's apartment, but Martin was at work. James and his girlfriend were there. When the assistant laid out what had happened, James knew something wasn't right. Meanwhile Cray was at the morgue, preparing to arrest Martin.

Katherine vanished and came to the morgue, to find Martin and Cray fighting. In turn, she found herself tied up on a table, and soon Martin was beside her.

James and Cray's assistant arrived, but Cray violently took them out of the picture—he'd gone way over the edge. As he prepared to dismember Martin and Katherine, James freed himself, and shot the Inspector. The ordeal was over, and along the way James also began to feel again, to regain himself.

There was very little gratuitous violence in the movie, but that didn't stop it from being a constant undercurrent, one that the director seemed to revel in and gleefully exploit. The English script had been written by director Bornedal and Steven Soderbergh (*sex, lies, & videotape*); perhaps it had just been Americanized from the Danish, but there was a real glorification of sickness in it.

Apart from Martin Bells and Inspector Cray, the characters were little more than ciphers, there just to fill up space and act as foils. Even James, Martin's catalyst, never seemed fully formed, and the part of Katherine was a complete waste of Patricia Arquette's talents.

The reservations Danny Boyle had had about Ewan's American accent after seeing scenes from this film were quite justified. On the surface it was fine, but the Scots burr kept creeping through. However, Ewan was quite convincing playing a student, looking fresh-faced and American, somewhat naive, and slowly realizing just how far out of his depth he was. And it was a pleasant change to have a male lead who was something of a wimp, a floater who went with the tide.

The person who stole the film, as much as anyone could, was Nolte, playing Cray. He hammed it up as the psychopathic cop, adding layers to his character as the plot moved along. Then again, he had the most complex role to play, unlike Martin Bells, who was open and straightforward—what you saw was what you got.

Certainly Ewan had been right to praise the cinematography, which was eerie, and also quite lovely at times, in contrast to the mood of the film.

All in all, it wasn't a great success for anyone concerned. Bornedal's American directorial debut, although meant to be a thriller, was palpably lacking in tension, and he seemed to be unable to draw excellent performances from anyone in his cast. The sheer blankness and vapidity of Martin Bells offered Ewan very little to work with, and though he tried valiantly, there was honestly little he could do.

It became easy to see—at least, see cynically—why Miramax delayed the film's release to try and cash in on Ewan's popularity after *A Life Less Ordinary*. On its own it would have been nothing, something that slipped in and out of the theaters in a week, drawing very few paying customers, and probably very few reviews—a B movie.

With Ewan's name attached, certainly after his higher profile and the films he'd signed to make, it would at least attract some attention, and the people who'd become Ewan's fans would troop out to see it—unfortunately, for all the wrong reasons. And it was notable that Ewan himself did little to promote the release, just letting it slide out. In fact, in the end it did come and go with very little fanfare at all, as if the studio realized it had very little hope right from the beginning.

It wasn't a critical smash, and the reviewers didn't fall over themselves to praise it, either. *Entertainment Weekly* (which had it listed by its working title of *The Late Shift*) called it "a horror for reasons that have nothing to do with suspenseful moviemaking," and "a post-*Seven* creative wasteland." *Rolling Stone* found fault with the Americanization of the story, saying that it "can't convince us that a big-city morgue harboring dark secrets could hold off the tabloids," and *Variety* compared it to "an intellectual 'snuff' movie."

The reviewers were mixed about Nolte's performance. *Variety* tagged him as "a lumbering, oblique presence who veers from the dimwitted to the sagacious without seeming benefit of drugs," while *Rolling Stone* had him "hammy enough to come garnished with pineapple."

Ewan did earn some plaudits, however. To Leonard Klady in *Variety*, he was "good and credible as the protagonist, but he mostly serves as the anchor of a rudderless ship." And *Rolling Stone* pointed out that it was "a taste for the twisted that promises a long career" for Ewan, while admitting that *Nightwatch* was about as twisted as anyone could reasonably imagine.

With that out of the way, the grimy taste of L.A.

washed out of his mouth, Ewan could move on to a project that was far more palatable. It was even one that was filmed close to home, so he could spend more time with the women in his life.

Eleven

Ewan had managed to become one of the busiest actors anywhere in the world. He had them stacked up like an air traffic controller, each one waiting for the right moment to come in to land. If there was any danger at all, it was that Ewan would be over-exposed. If he liked the script and the director, he added it to his list, until he was forced to admit, "Yeah, I've got to say no, but I am not very good at that. I'm just not very good at that."

One project that received an unconditional 'yes' from him was *Velvet Goldmine*. Directed by Todd Haynes, who'd made something of an underground splash with his controversial film *Poison* (1991), and produced by Michael Stipe, the singer for REM, this was exactly the kind of thing to thrill Ewan.

He'd never lost the love of music that he'd had as a teenager in Crieff, back when he was the drummer for Scarlet Pride. He didn't really play any more, apart from the occasional few seconds at the drum kit on film (although he still had his own drum set and an electric guitar at home, and harbored the occasional fantasy of starting a band), but music still moved him—in particular, the music of the Britpop band Oasis, who'd become globally successful. As he admitted, "I've really got a teen-age thing about Oasis. I'm really silly about them."

Velvet Goldmine was set in the early 1970s in England, a film that was centered around the whole glam-rock era that produced stars like David Bowie and Roxy Music. When Ewan was offered the chance to play Curt Wild in the movie, an American who moved to London seeking success in the music business, it was irresistible. With Haynes's reputation, he knew it would be gritty, and Stipe's involvement would mean that the production had both integrity and authenticity.

"It's so brilliantly put together," Ewan said before filming began. "It's fractured, with loads of scenes without dialogue, and other scenes which are just snippets."

Best of all, it would give Ewan a chance to live out his long-held fantasy of being a rock star, in what he called "the amphetamine-fueled seventies"—and get paid for it. He was in good company, working alongside Toni Collette (whom he'd met when they were both part of the cast of *Emma*), Irishman Jonathan Rhys-Meyers, who was an actor on the rise in Britain, Christian Bale, Eddie Izzard, and Linsay Kemp, the man who, in the 1960s, taught David Bowie about movement and mime.

Ewan's portrayal of Wild was based loosely on Iggy Pop ("legally I have to say a kind of Iggy Pop," he explained), the Detroit rocker who'd first become known in 1969 with the Stooges. Onstage, Iggy had definitely been wild, cutting himself on the chest with broken bottles, insulting the audience and inviting them to beat him up. His music, first with the Stooges, then later as a solo artist, had largely foreshadowed the punk era of the mid-seventies, and the punks saw him as something of a godfather of the movement.

Pop also become something of a protege of David Bowie, after Bowie had become a superstar, and in 1977 Bowie produced Iggy's album, *The Idiot*, as well as playing keyboards and joining him on tour.

The real Iggy Pop had never attempted to forge a glam-rock career for himself in London. In fact, his early albums, sloppy and squalling, were almost the antithesis of the relatively slick glam. But over the years his musical reputation (and the mere fact of his survival) had made him an iconic figure. For the first part of his career, he'd been as famous for his outrageous behavior, often dropping his pants onstage, as the music he made. There were some states he wasn't able to return to for many years because of outstanding arrest warrants.

Iggy was the perfect model for the fictional Curt Wild. In one part of the film, a concert sequence with Wild onstage before a crowd of four hundred, Ewan was able to improvise his performance and ended up dropping his own pants, exposing himself and insulting the audience.

"I was so into it," he admitted. "I end up naked and showing off my [body] again." It could never be said that Ewan was shy about showing his body, just like Iggy. "I watch a lot of Iggy [on video]," Ewan admitted. "He's like a small kid, thrashing around in sporadic bursts, not even in time with the music sometimes. It's like he has to let it all out. Having experience doing that in front of two hundred extras, I know that's the key to this character."

To play the role, Ewan wore blond, shoulder-length wigs, leaving him looking not unlike the late

Kurt Cobain of Nirvana, and applied plenty of makeup.

"I love it!" Ewan said of his appearance. "I keep saying, 'More eyeliner! More!' The makeup artist puts it on and I spend several minutes rubbing it around." As well as the wigs and makeup, his clothing consisted of "leather trousers and hipster flares. I'm quite grungy."

One aspect of the movie that didn't worry him at all was the simulated gay love scene he had to film with co-star Christian Bale (playing a music journalist), where their characters have sex. In fact, the filming of that scene gave rise to a humorous anecdote from Ewan: "In one scene, I come off-stage and [Bale is] in the wings there, and I take him onto this rooftop and we have sex." The filming seemed to last a suspiciously long time, and Ewan and Bale began to wonder what was happening. "Finally, I said, 'Well, I'm gonna look.' 'Cause Christian couldn't figure it out either. And I looked on the rooftop and people were just pickin' up the tracks, and cables and wires and they just never said, 'Cut.' They hadn't bothered to stop us."

For many stars with heartthrob reputations and a strong female fan base, such a scene would have been completely off-limits. However, it was typical of Ewan that he wouldn't follow the standard star mentality. He'd accepted the role as it was written. If scenes like that were a part of the character and the story, he had no qualms about playing them. After all, he'd done it before, in *The Pillow Book*. The people who came to the theater to see him act would see Ewan as the character, not Ewan being Ewan. If they had a problem with his character's sexuality, that was unfortunate, but they needed to separate the fiction from the fact.

As much as Ewan enjoyed filming parts of the movie, and playing Curt Wild, in the end the shoot proved to be somewhat frustrating for him. Although he'd loved the script, in the finished product too many of the scenes, he felt, were brief, and never made their point. At the same time, how many movies would give him the opportunity to live out that rock-star fantasy? For all his eventual doubts about what ended up onscreen, it wasn't an experience he would have missed.

The title *Velvet Goldmine*, came from a lyric on David Bowie's *The Rise and Fall of Ziggy Stardust and the Spiders from Mars*, as seminal a glam record as there was. Jonathan Rhys-Meyers played Brian Slade, a character who wasn't David Bowie, but who possessed more than a few parallels with the rock star. Slade had blue spiked hair (Bowie's at that time was a spiky orange feather cut), and both were bisexual (Bowie had "come out" in the press as a bisexual in 1971); in fact, in the movie, Slade expressed sexual interest in Ewan's character of Curt Wild.

The story was told in flashback, beginning in the eighties, when Bale's journalist character asked Slade's wife, Mandy (played by Toni Collette), to tell her husband's story, after he faked his death and disappeared.

Ewan's films with the troika of Boyle, MacDonald, and Hodge had been marked by the way music had been an integral part of the cinematic experience, reaching a high point in *Trainspotting*. *Velvet Goldmine* would offer something similar, and not just because it was set in the music world. With

REM's Michael Stipe not only producing but also supervising the music, the stage was set, through his connections, to get the best. And that included Lou Reed's "Satellite of Love," from his breakthrough 1972 album, *Transformer*, which was produced by Bowie and Bowie's guitarist, the late Mick Ronson. Also lined up were Radiohead, covering period material by Roxy Music, and Placebo, doing a version of Marc Bolan's (T. Rex) 1970s song "20th Century Boy."

One thing the soundtrack wouldn't have, however, was a David Bowie song; he'd refused permission for any of his material to be used in the film, with a spokesperson for the artist simply saying, "The rights to David Bowie's music are not available to the makers of *Velvet Goldmine*," although it was speculated in the British press that Bowie might have been keeping the songs for a *Ziggy Stardust* revival tour.

The film had originally been scheduled to open in the spring of 1998. However, some of the negatives had been accidentally destroyed in the editing process, which meant that the premiere had to be pushed back. It finally received its first public airing at the Cannes Film Festival, in May 1998, where it won a Special Jury Prize for Artistic Contribution. Reuters gave the film a glowing review, noting that "McGregor is perfectly brilliant as the charismatic and heroin-addicted Wild, delivering concert performances worthy of the best rock idols." From there, the film's next appearance was set for the Toronto Film Festival, in September, before a full American release in November.

Ewan, however, hard at work on yet another film, wasn't in attendance at Cannes. He was, however, well represented. Not only was he one of the stars of *Velvet Goldmine*, but he was in *The Serpent's Kiss*, which was also receiving its first showing at the festival.

Directed by Philippe Rousselot, who had a long career as a cinematographer (*A River Runs Through It*), it saw Ewan teaming up again with two actors he'd worked with before—Pete Postlethwaite (*Brassed Off*) and Greta Scacchi (*Emma*).

In England, in 1699, Thomas Smithers (Postlethwaite) decided to have his garden landscaped. It wasn't just any garden, but an estate, for Smithers was a rich man, an aristocrat, with a beautiful wife (Scacchi). He hired an eminent young Dutch landscape artist, Meneer Chrome (Ewan), to design and oversee the work. Chrome, however, was not what he seemed; The person going under that name wasn't the real Chrome at all, but an imposter, seeking to succeed as a landscaper.

The plot became convoluted. Smithers' wife fell for the fake Chrome, and he, in his turn, fell for Smithers daughter (Carmen Chaplin). In a series of twists, another man attempted to blackmail Chrome into ruining Smithers. In the end, however, everyone lived happily ever after.

The judges at Cannes weren't as kind to this entry as they'd been to *Velvet Goldmine*; it came away without any prizes. In point of fact, it came away without much praise. In its review of the Cannes showing, *Cinemotion* called it "an astonishingly naked rip-off of [Peter Greenaway's] *The Draughtsman's Contract*, noting that the characters "wander about inanely, engaged in wooden dialogue from a terrifically bad script. This Greenaway-for-idiots marks a nadir of sorts for the festival." The best that could be said for Ewan was that he was ''miscast.''

That didn't bode well for the film's future at the box office, although it was hard to believe that actors of the caliber of Ewan, Postlethwaite, and Scacchi could turn in work that was anything less than wonderful.

Playing a rock star was something close to Ewan's secret heart. From there, however, he had to make a 180-degree turn for his next role, *Rogue Trader*, and the world of very high finance.

Nick Leeson had begun life as a working-class child, growing up in Watford, not far from London. After finishing his education, he'd gone to work for Baring's, an English merchant bank that had been founded in 1763, a place where ''gentlemen'' did their business, money changed hands in a quiet and civilized fashion, and many millions of pounds were made annually.

Leeson moved quite swiftly through the ranks, even though he didn't have the kind of moneyed or aristocratic background generally associated with merchant bankers. What worked in his favor was the fact that he was very good at his job. Still in his twenties, he was promoted, and made the general manager of Baring's Singapore branch.

Along with Hong Kong, which was still a British Crown Colony (it reverted to China in 1997), Singapore was Asia's financial center, with a stock exchange and strong international trading connections. To be the general manager of a respected merchant bank there was an extremely responsible position, and Leeson was soon moving money around on behalf of his employers, with very profitable results.

The head office in London gave Leeson free rein in his dealings. Unfortunately, not all of them were good, and in time he began manipulating balances, to make his trading appear profitable, when, in fact, it was vastly in the red. The losses he was sustaining were huge, and growing bigger every day.

Finally, in 1995, the deception was discovered. Leeson disappeared, eventually being arrested in Germany, then extradited to Singapore, where he was convicted of fraud and sentenced to jail. On examination, it was discovered that the losses he'd managed to hide totaled more than $1 billion, and brought about the economic collapse of Baring's bank. It was thought—and still is by some—that Leeson hadn't lost the money, but had embezzled it, although that was never proved.

Leeson wrote his autobiography, and the rights were bought by English television personality Sir David Frost, who had interviewed Leeson after his arrest in Germany. The financing came, as was often the case with British movies, from a British television company, in this case Granada.

"It was plain as a pikestaff, this was a wonderful story," Frost said. However, friends of his involved in the City didn't seem to think so, and Frost reported he received calls which said, "David, I don't think it would help anybody if you do a film about Nick Leeson."

Having made up his mind, secured the rights, and arranged the financing, Frost wasn't about to let himself be dissuaded at this point. Writer James Dearden, who'd penned the hit movie *Fatal Attraction* (1987), and who was also a director, with credits including 1991's *A Kiss Before Dying*, was hired to write and direct the movie.

Brought in to star as Leeson was none other than Ewan, although he quickly learned that he wouldn't have liked the intense life of a financier.

"I couldn't hack it for five minutes," he admitted simply.

Nor did he make an attempt to visit Leeson in his Singapore jail as part of his research for the role. "I'd have been embarrassed," Ewan reasoned. "What would I say? 'Hi, I'm playing you in a movie—and you're rotting away in jail.' It would be awful." He did, however, hope to meet Leeson at the eventual London premiere, by which time Leeson should be a free man.

"This was a guy with an intriguing dilemma," Ewan said. "He started making these massive losses, but what choice did he have but to carry on? The more I learn about him, the more he comes to fascinate me."

Perhaps because of the fact that it dealt with extremely large amounts of money, the kind of environment where the players were essentially gamblers wagering very high stakes, Ewan admitted that there was a definite glamor to the film.

"Though I don't think because I'm in it, it's necessarily glamorous," he added. "But this film is based on [Leeson's] book, which is bound to glamorize him. You could choose not to make a film based on his book—but that would be a different kind of film."

Both Ewan and his co-star, Anna Friel, best known for her work on the British television soap opera, *Brookside* (she would be playing Leeson's wife, Lisa) had modified their accents. Friel's hard

Lancashire vowels had softened, Ewan had lost his normal Scots burr, and they'd taken on approximately neutral English accents. For once, Ewan wore his bangs combed forward, giving him a more youthful look, and appearing engagingly honest—the perfect Leeson.

Ewan was certainly happy to have been offered the role, and to have been able to play a man so obsessed by success that he'd do anything, even commit a crime, to make himself appear that way.

"I feel it's the most acting I've done for a long time," he said. "There's a lot to get my teeth into."

And, for most of the shoot, he didn't even have to travel far, just to Pinewood Studios (little more than a few minutes from his North London home), where the designers had built a replica of the trading floor of SIMEX, the Singapore International Money Exchange. There, as Leeson, he strode around the floor, through piles of discarded paper—trading slips—looked at the flashing computer screens, and made his bids with all the other traders, every one of them (including Ewan) dressed in loudly striped jackets.

It was a long way from the junkie squats and seedy drug deals of Edinburgh, but in some ways it plumbed similar basic human emotions. Like so many of the characters Ewan had played—Robert, Martin Bells, Alex, but most particularly Mark Renton—Nick Leeson was a man who found himself in over his head. The difference was that Renton could—and did—clean up his act and change his life. For Leeson, there was absolutely no way he could repay the huge loss he'd hidden with creative bookkeeping; it was bound to be discovered eventually. The best he could do was run until he was caught.

Once his work on that was in the can, it was time for Ewan to fly to Canada, to begin shooting *Eye of the Beholder*, a thriller, which had Ewan as its star, along with Ashley Judd (*Ruby in Paradise*, *A Time to Kill*), the acting member of the Judd country music family. It also starred singer k. d. lang, who had previously appeared on screen in *Salmonberries* and *The Last Don*, as well as Jason Priestley (*Beverly Hills 90210*) and Patrick Bergin. (According to the English *Daily Mail*, the film was also set to star Jeanne Tripplehorn (*The Firm, Waterworld, Sliding Doors*). It would be directed by Stephen Elliott, who'd made something of a splash with *Priscilla, Queen of the Desert*. The filming began March 23, 1998, in Montreal. It was a high-tech thriller—a very definite change of pace for Ewan—about a detective who was tracking a female serial killer.

As if all that weren't quite enough for one man, there was also *Nora*, in which he was cast as James Joyce, the Irish author (*Ulysses, Finnegan's Wake*) who moved to Paris, where he did his most important work. The Nora of the title was Nora Barnacle, who met Joyce in Ireland in 1902. They became lovers, and when Joyce left Ireland for good, Nora accompanied him. They never married, something which was quite scandalous in those days, although they lived as man and wife, and Nora bore Joyce's two children, a boy and a girl.

After *Nora* was *The Rise and Fall of Little Voice*, and then, reportedly, *The Hellfire Club*. But rumors abounded about new Ewan movies. One had him as a cast member of *eXistenZ*, an upcoming project from director David Cronenberg (*Crash*, *Naked Lunch*), along with David Thewlis, Jennifer Jason Leigh, and a whole host of up-and-coming young British actors, known collectively as members of the "Brit Pack": Sean Pertwee (with whom Ewan had acted in *Bluejuice*), Sadie Frost, and Jonny Lee Miller (Sick Boy from *Trainspotting*). Another rumor had him signing to make *South From Hell's Kitchen*, with Bridget Fonda as his co-star. None of the rumors gained any quick confirmation, however.

They didn't need to. With Ewan's work ethic, it was quite believable that he had agreed to be in every one, and probably a few more besides. However, the movie that Ewan's fans—not to mention many millions more around the globe—were waiting for already had a release date set: Memorial Day, 1999.

Twelve

The *Star Wars* trilogy—*Star Wars* (1977), *The Empire Strikes Back* (1980), and *Return of the Jedi* (1983)—had not only been phenomenally successful at the box office, they'd also become cultural icons for the generation that grew up waiting in line to see them in the theaters, and those younger who were only exposed to them on video. When they were given a second theatrical release in 1997, with the sound and visuals carefully remastered, and a few extra scenes added, the response was phenomenal, grossing $251 million in the U.S. alone.

The trilogy had set a new standard for special effects, almost light years ahead of anything that had gone before. Even though the story was archetypal good against evil, David taking on Goliath, its science fiction setting made it timeless, as did the characters themselves—Luke Skywalker, Princess Leia, Darth Vader, Obi Wan Kenobi. Their names became part of everyday language.

Star Wars was also one of the first movies to have a massive marketing campaign tied into it, as action figures and all manner of toys, officially licensed, hit the stores to coincide with the release. And they found their mark. Kids everywhere, enthralled by the film, went out to buy all the items they could, and re-enact scenes from the film. Two decades later, tied in with the films' re-release, another $4 billion of merchandise was sold.

Star Wars set new standards in everything—effects, box office receipts, and influence. After the trilogy, virtually every action film had to up the ante on special effects, to the point where they didn't just enhance the action, but largely became it, and production costs spiralled upwards in ridiculous fashion.

Ewan was six years old when *Star Wars* was released, and he immediately fell in love with it, not just for the film itself (although, like all young boys, he found the action impossible to resist), but because his uncle, Denis Lawson, was a member of the cast. Lawson played Wedge, the X-Wing fighter pilot, a role he'd also take in both sequels.

To him it wasn't merely great filmmaking, it was something that could transport him back to when he was young, a big part of his childhood, of innocence and enthusiasm, when movies were just beginning to exert their influence on him.

For a long time, director George Lucas had been promising another trilogy of films, the "prequels" to *Star Wars*. Rumor had originally circulated that they'd be made right after *Return of the Jedi*, but that had never happened. The idea continued to circulate from time to time. While most fans lived in hope of it happening, few honestly believed it would.

Then, remarkably, the rumors and hopes all came true. Lucas announced that *Star Wars: The Balance of the Force* would be released in 1999, with the second and third parts—tentatively titled *The Rise of the Empire* and *The Fall of the Jedi*, scheduled for 2001 and 2003, respectively.

To call them the most highly anticipated films in history wouldn't have been an overstatement. Lucas would direct *Star Wars: The Balance of the Force*, but announced early that he would not be behind the camera for the other two films, although it seemed likely that Steven Spielberg would direct the second part.

It would have been perfectly understandable if Lucas had wanted to make these movies bigger and better than anything that had preceded them. Instead, his object was to keep costs for each film below the $100 million mark that seemed to separate movie from blockbuster. He'd invested $150 million of his own money into the production of the three; he wasn't simply gambling with someone else's cash, although plenty of people would have been happy to give it to him.

To help keep costs down, and speed up the entire production process, all the interiors for the prequels were shot at Leavesden Studios, just outside London, after the exteriors had been shot in Tunisia (the location-filming for the other two films would be combined in one long nine-month shoot at the millennium). At the close of work each day, all the footage was sent through fiber-optic cables to Industrial Light and Magic, the famous special-effects studio that Lucas owned in San Rafael, California. Since that was eight hours behind England, while the actors and crew slept, technicians could weave their own particular spells on the action, saving a great deal of money—and time.

A huge amount of secrecy shrouded the entire film. The script was guarded like a state secret. It was obvious to fans, however, that the story would follow the rise of Emperor Palpatine and the fall of the Republic and its Jedi Knights. Everyone involved had to sign confidentiality agreements, including cinematographer David Tattersall, who said, "No telling what they'd do to me if I talked."

While fans murmured about the script, speculating on the details of the story as they waited anxiously, the other big question was who would be in the films? Mark Hamill, Carrie Fisher, and Harrison Ford would not be returning, that much was obvious, but exactly who would be there?

The word managed to leak out, even before contracts were finalized. Liam Neeson would be a Jedi master, supervisor of twelve young knights. The young Anakin Skywalker, the boy who'd grow up to become Darth Vader, was eight-year-old Jake Lloyd, who'd been seen before in *Jingle All the Way*. Sixteen-year-old Natalie Portman, whose biggest role had been in *The Professional*, was set to be the Young Queen, who'd fall in love with the future Darth, and marry him in the second part, before giving birth to the twins Luke and Leia. Samuel L. Jackson (*Pulp Fiction, Jackie Brown*) would have a cameo.

The plum role, however, had to be that of Ben Kenobi, the man who'd eventually earn the title of Obi-Wan, and guide Luke in the Force. Obviously, the idea of Sir Alec Guinness coming back was out of the question. Someone much younger was needed, and all manner of names were bandied around, including Kenneth Branagh. In the end, however, the producers turned to Ewan.

To those familiar with his work, it seemed odd

that he'd take the part. After all, he'd been very vocal in his criticism of blockbusters.

"I don't think of [the *Star Wars* pictures] as event movies," he explained. "It's not like being in *Robocop 5* or something. The *Star Wars* movies are way beyond studio pictures. They're enormous. I can't say no."

And it would offer some family continuity. He'd been six when he first saw his uncle in the original *Star Wars*. Ewan's daughter, Clara, would be six when the second of the prequels appeared.

The Balance of the Force, as Ewan rightly pointed out, was far more than just another Hollywood blockbuster. As *Star Wars* had defined movies for one generation, this would do it for another. Becoming part of the fabric of popular culture—on a global scale—was something no one could turn down. But there was another reason for Ewan's acceptance of the role of Ben Kenobi.

"I see doing the three *Star Wars* movies as a way out of having to do major blockbusters. I don't have to do another." And, he added elsewhere, "There's nothing cooler than a Jedi Knight."

As it was, though, Ewan *did* almost almost turn down the role. Boyle, MacDonald, and Hodge, his favorite people in the film business, had asked him to read for a part in their new project, *The Beach*, which, according to Boyle, was "a kind of commitment on our part."

For a while it looked as if the shooting schedules for *The Beach* and *Star Wars: The Balance of the Force* might conflict, "and I wouldn't have done *Star Wars* if that was the case, if they'd offered me this," said Ewan. "And that was completely clear in my mind."

In the end, filming of *The Beach* was put back several months, and so the choice became unnecessary. Still, it was an indication of the regard in which Ewan held the troika, that he would have been willing to turn his back on such a thing. As he explained, *Star Wars* was "a very different thing for me, but it's not ultimately what I'm about in terms of an actor in films and stuff."

It was a level of integrity very rare in show business. Certainly he wasn't doing the *Star Wars* films for the money; with their relatively limited budgets, Ewan wouldn't be getting rich—at least not Hollywood rich—off the series, but then he'd never undertaken anything solely for the money. The experiences and memories would be worth a fortune, although, he joked, his real dream was "to play Princess Leia. Stick some big pastries on my head. Now *that* would be interesting."

Unfortunately, it was also highly unlikely.

And he was in such an established position as an actor that he didn't need to ponder the fates of the leads of the original *Star Wars* trilogy. Of them only Harrison Ford's career had continued onward and upward, while both Mark Hamill and Carrie Fisher found themselves forever associated with their characters from a galaxy far, far away. With his track record, Ewan would never have to worry about typecasting. He'd already escaped the straitjacket of Renton, and the roles he played were so varied that there seemed to be no danger of Ben Kenobi acting like a millstone around his neck for the rest of his life.

The first thing he had to do for the part was watch old Alec Guinness films, when Guinness was a young man, to achieve some approximation of the voice, and try to see himself as one of Britain's great actors. However, he didn't approach Sir Alec and ask for advice.

"What would I say?" Ewan wondered. " 'How'd you do it?' He's only in half the first movie, and it's a legendary performance."

The trick, he decided, was in the voice.

"I have to get his accent. He's got this very specific older man's voice. It'd be great if I could trace it back to his youth and get it right."

But there were other things he'd need for the role, and his most important prop would be his light saber. Amazingly, he was offered a choice.

"It's the most secretive thing," he said in surprise. "I have to sign papers. This guy looked me in the eye and said, 'Are you ready?' Then he opened up a briefcase-sized box with eight or nine light-saber handles. I picked the sexiest one. I realized, I've been waiting twenty years to have my own light saber."

But he couldn't reveal what it looked like. He wasn't even allowed to say what color it was. That was the kind of importance given to everything involved with this project.

Ewan was able to say, however, that more than two decades hadn't seen much of an improvement in the dialogue. A lot of it was still awkward and stilted.

"There's some *choice* lines, yeah. Everything is very deliberate—it's all about 'We're gonna do *this* now,' as opposed to what you're thinking. So the key is to just get it out."

But *Star Wars* had never been about acting ability or quality of dialogue. It was about the story, which was bigger than any single actor. Besides, what could Ewan have done about it? "What am I going to say?" he wondered. "George, your dialogue's [terrible]?"

The audience wouldn't be caring about how good or bad the words were; it was the spectacle of the thing that mattered. Lucas had taken an old idea and transformed it into one of the great epics of the late twentieth century. Ewan understood that completely, and he was simply happy to be a part of it, to pick up the torch from his uncle, and keep the family tradition alive.

He was doing these films for Denis Lawson, for himself, and for Clara, to give her something she could watch and be proud of her father, the way Ewan had been proud of his uncle. And, whether consciously or not, he was doing them for the ages. Prior to this, his name and *Trainspotting* had gone together like peanut butter and jelly. After Memorial Day, 1999, he would be associated with Ben Kenobi for the rest of his days. No matter what else he did, how good or how bad, the tag would remain, because the films, like their predecessors, would be cultural landmarks. They'd affect entire generations of kids—and adults. The young Ben Kenobi would be Ewan's giant contribution to the industry of human happiness. And, in turn, it would turn him from an actor into a household name, something he didn't really want to contemplate, but which he knew in his heart would be true.

At the same time, it would set him completely free, to make any film he wanted on his name alone. It would simply be that huge. When the first *Star Wars* movie appeared in 1977, it had defined the idea of blockbuster, both in its special effects, and in box office. Since then the stakes had risen, and there had been plenty of films that cost over $200 million to make. But there was one line that hadn't been crossed, that stood like a holy grail in front of filmmakers—to take in $100 million in a film's opening weekend.

It was a stupendous amount of money, largely unimaginable for most people. But such was the power of the *Star Wars* myth, and the anticipation for this new film—which, after all, was the first in the series for sixteen years—that some industry insiders confidently believed that *The Balance of the Force* could break that barrier.

However much money it brought in, and how many more billions (and they would be billions) of dollars came from all the merchandise, was of little interest to Ewan. By the time any film was released, it was history to him. He'd moved on and completed one, two, possibly even three more projects. He couldn't even consider the idea of his face on action figures and posters, because that wasn't him; it was Ben Kenobi. Ewan McGregor was the guy who found that "*Star Wars* was great fun to do," but who saw it as another role, a way to escape the threat of Hollywood, rather than as a pinnacle in his career. Yes, it was special, but in the end it was just another part, not life or death.

How he saw it all was one thing; the perception of the public was another. After *Trainspotting*, Ewan had become a very public face in Britain. He wanted anonymity in his private life, but he found himself stopped by fans for pictures and autographs. In the wake of *Star Wars*, everything that had gone before would be very small potatoes. Like it or not, international celebrity was waiting just around the corner for Ewan.

Thirteen

It's hard to believe that Ewan's real film career is only five years old; it was just in 1994 that he astonished audiences and critics for the first time with his performance in *Shallow Grave*. Or that by then he'd only been acting professionally for a year.

Very few people have done as much in as short a time. He's filmed a staggering 17 movies, more than three a year, running the entire gamut of acting possibilities, from criminal junkie to rock star to nineteenth-century dandy to Jedi Knight. It's been a life very much less ordinary, and one which has allowed him hardly any time off.

His star has risen, and just keeps on rising and rising, until he's like to become that champagne supernova that he sang about at his friend's wedding.

Along the way, he's also managed to sustain a real life, to woo and marry Eve, and to help raise their daughter, as well as shield them from the spotlight of publicity that always seems to be trained on him. It's been a remarkable balancing act between the public and private Ewans, but he's managed it with ease. Ewan and Eve don't indulge Clara; they've kept her away from the pervasive influence of television (''it's much better for her to look at books''); if she's allowed to watch something, it's a video of the British children's show, *Pingu*.

He still lives quite unpretentiously in London, popping out to his local pub for a drink just like many other men in the neighborhood. Off the set he's Ewan, regular guy, not Ewan, the star. And off the set he still enjoys being around his mates, and having a good time.

"I'm married and have a kid, but I'm certainly not settled down. I like going out and [Eve] likes staying home. So there's some balance there," he laughed. "Also a lot of arguments." But absolutely no doubt that Ewan is devoted to his family.

Fame has allowed him to indulge one of his passions—motorcycles. He owns a Moto Guzzi, and recently acquired a new Ducati, which he bought for $21,000. "I imported it from Italy, and it's absolutely stunning," he said with pride.

Fame has also brought him into contact with other famous people, not just actors, but musicians, something to relish for the man who has never quite got over the desire to be a rock'n'roll star. One good friend is Gavin Rossdale, the lead singer of Bush; when they play in London, Ewan will invariably be backstage.

But the awe of a famous man is reserved for one of the biggest bands in the world—Oasis.

"I have a very teenage thing about Oasis," he's admitted sheepishly. And he's preached about their music like any other infatuated teenager. When their album *Be Here Now* was released in 1997, he gave copies to all the cast and crew of *Star Wars*, but only after listening to it alone at home on headphones, scared that he might not enjoy it. There was even a glowing review, supposedly penned by Ewan (although he denied writing it) printed in the British newspaper *The Sun*.

He also vocally defended them in interviews, the way any teenage boy would defend his favorite band: "Old [Beatle] George Harrison was slagging [their album] off today saying it's okay if you're fourteen, but it's rubbish really, and I was thinking, wait a minute, what's wrong with a fourteen-year-old's taste in music? How dare he?"

But when he wants to see them perform, he doesn't have to wait in line for tickets like a teenager. Instead, there's the VIP treatment, backstage passes, and invitations to the party after the gig. Celebrity does have its compensations. . . .

Not that Ewan needs compensations. His life couldn't have gone any better if he'd dreamed it this way. He's one of the busiest actors in England, being offered the plum roles, and still too eager to work to refuse any of them. Still, he looks ahead to when he'll have a real break.

"I've got a [motorcycle] trip planned for when I've got the time, when I slow down a bit. I want to go from [England] to Holland, then go through France, down through Italy and over to Africa and go round North Africa. . . . It would only take about six to eight weeks. . . . I'd like to just do it on my own, I think. I like riding on my own."

A vacation like that would be a first for him; the biggest question is whether he'd be willing to take that much time off. He's said before that he'd "go mad" if he had six whole months off, with nothing to do. He's driven, as he's admitted, a true workaholic who only finds real satisfaction from life when he's acting for the cameras.

Along the way, he's produced some astonishing performances. As Mark Renton he managed to define the essence of British hipness in 1996—not for Renton's junkie habits, but his attitude, cynicism, and humor. *Brassed Off*'s Andy was a fully rounded portrait of a Yorkshireman experiencing so many emotions, and culturally unable to talk about any of them, a man who saw his future imploding and, at the same time, expanding with possibilities. In *The Pillow Book*, it was his body, not so much him, that was the character, and he played it with grace and dignity, exploring himself, and literally dying for love. Robert, in *A Life Less Ordinary*, was the archetypal loser who became a winner, the charming bungler who seemed to let life happen to him, only finding his redemption in romance—the complete opposite of *Emma*'s Frank Churchill.

The secret has been finding bits of each character within himself, and letting them come out in his work. Acting is a kind of magic spell, one woven in front of an audience, to make them believe that what they're seeing is real. And Ewan has proved to be a powerful wizard.

But it's something he doesn't need to carry over into the everyday world of going out for a drink, or driving to the supermarket to do the shopping. As he's said so often, he doesn't need to subscribe to the Method style of acting, living his part 24 hours a day. When he leaves the set the mask is removed, and he's completely himself again.

One thing that seems certain about Ewan's career is that he'll continue to work with Danny Boyle, John Hodge, and Andrew MacDonald.

"I just want to work with them," he said. "I

love it, I love it. It'd be weird if I wasn't ever to do another film with them.''

It does seem that Boyle has the knack for bringing out the best performances from him, the ones that do full justice to his prodigious talent. Ewan has, in a way, become the fourth member of the team, fully committed to what they're doing—anyone who'd have turned down *Star Wars: The Balance of the Force* to work with them is obviously loyal!

But that team can only make one film at a time, and there's plenty of work needed after the shooting has finished. Which means that, while Ewan would happily work with them every week, year in, year out, he can't, and so he fills his time with other projects.

It's Boyle, Hodge, and MacDonald who made his name known, who gave him the role of a lifetime in *Trainspotting*, but it's Ewan's talent that's brought him to stardom.

Trainspotting was, beyond any doubt, the key to everything, the turning point in Ewan's career. Before that he was just another young actor, one face among many. He had good credits to his name, mainly in television, but so did plenty of others. Even *Shallow Grave* hadn't singled him out (both Kerry Fox and Christopher Eccleston were outstanding in that film, but neither of them is in the new *Star Wars* trilogy, for example), beyond being a talent to watch. As Mark Renton, Ewan hit a zeitgeist. Thanks to bands like Oasis and Blur, Britpop was resurgent all over the globe. There was a hunger for things British, which *Trainspotting*, with perfect timing, fed into. It was hip and cynical, and Renton was the perfect anti-hero. However unlike his character Ewan was in real life, he played the role so well that to audiences, he *was* Renton. And, rightly or wrongly, that made him the hippest, coolest actor to come out of the British Isles since the sixties. The film was so successful, striking a chord in a generation and beyond, that it made Ewan into an international name in one fell swoop. It might possibly have happened to anyone who'd played that part; it's impossible to speculate. But Ewan made Renton likeable, invested him with a charm and charisma that was impossible to resist. And from then on, Ewan was set. But in reality, that was only one stop in his development as an actor.

From *Shallow Grave* to *A Life Less Ordinary* it was possible to see him grow on the screen, improving by leaps and bounds with each new appearance, becoming more assured and commanding, until he'd really taken on the mantle of an actor who was also a star—a vast difference from someone who is only a star.

He's earned his stardom, he's worked incredibly hard for it, even if it was never his ultimate aim. In America, to be sure, he's not a household name, no Bruce Willis or Tom Hanks. But in Britain the name of Ewan McGregor is every bit as well known as those two, and far more respected. He's the local lad who's never wanted to sell out, to run after the almighty dollar for its own sake. He's been involved with two of the best films to come out of Britain in the last decade, and that's earned him respect, while his looks and the inherent attitudes of his characters have brought him plenty of female admiration.

Someone just pursuing stardom would have taken advantage of that, and just taken roles to increase his image. Not Ewan. A good role is a good role. In his own mind, there is no image to maintain. He's an actor, pure and simple. If he was concerned solely with image and appealing to women, he wouldn't have played the gay Curt Wild in *Velvet Goldmine*; in fact, he probably wouldn't have been involved in such an independent production at all.

To Americans, Ewan might seem like a bit of a rebel, one who wants to buck the Hollywood system. But he understands full well how people get sucked in and spat out of the star-making machinery, and that's not something he wants to buy into. Nor does he need to. The satisfaction comes from doing the work, not how much he's paid for it. Better a good role that pays $50,000, or even less (like the $7000 he received for being Mark Renton) than $5,000,000 to take part in a blockbuster he hated. It wouldn't even be a contest; he'd turn down the blockbuster.

So where does he go from here? He's now been involved with what will undoubtedly be one of the biggest movies in history, and he'll be in both the sequels. He's a major global player. The answer is, he'll go wherever he wants. Ewan will continue to chart the course he's always sailed, working with Boyle, Hodge, and MacDonald whenever possible, continuing to work mostly in Britain, where his reputation as Ben Kenobi won't count for anywhere near as much, and veering between independent films and low-budget studio productions.

The *Star Wars* films, as he intends, will allow him to escape the pressures of Hollywood breathing down his neck, making him ridiculous offers to star in ridiculous films. To the studios, from the moment he appears with his light saber, he'll be typecast; and if they're that blinkered, it suits him fine. He doesn't need them.

There's always going to be plenty of work for him, as much as he wants to take on, although he can't carry on indefinitely, making the number of films he has been doing. At first it was all an opportunity to prove himself, and for a starving young actor to earn a living. But he's moved beyond that stage now. He's established, and though he's certainly not wealthy by American standards, he's not struggling to make ends meet, either. Soon there'll come a break, maybe to take that motorcycle trip he's promised himself, or simply to spend some time at home, watching Clara grow, getting to know her properly. Ewan might even find that he likes a slightly less demanding schedule.

One thing that definitely won't vanish, however, is his desire to take chances with his craft. There'll be more films like *The Pillow Book* in the future, or like *Velvet Goldmine*, where he gets to challenge himself and go to extremes. Extremes are something that appeal to him, be it in weather—he prefers sandstorms or snow blizzards to a normal, sunny day—or films, which might have been one of the reasons that attracted him to the rather grotesque *Nightwatch*.

One extreme to which Ewan did push himself occured at the end of 1998, when he made his professional debut on the stage. Although he'd taken part in many productions during his student days, since leaving the Guildhall, Ewan's career had been exclusively in films and television. He'd been persuaded to tread the boards as a pro by none other than his uncle, and first acting influence, Denis Lawson, who was set to direct the play. They'd be performing David Halliwell's *Little Malcolm and His Struggle Against the Eunuchs*, which had been released in a cinematic version in 1974, starring John Hurt, under the title *Little Malcolm*. The play, surprisingly, wasn't going to be a major West End production. Instead it would be performed at the small, informal Hampstead Theatre Club, in Hampstead, a rich northwest suburb of London, running from November 18 to December 23.

There will also be more little gems like *Brassed Off*, and cameos when he has the time or the inclination—he'd probably jump at the offer to appear in an Oasis video. In fact, Ewan did continue his association with rock'n'roll when he narrated a documentary about the young Irish group, Ash, who sang the title track for *A Life Less Ordinary*. He'll grow older with grace, but he'll never grow old.

Without even trying, without even *wanting* to be, Ewan McGregor is hip. He stands slightly to the left of the mainstream, shuffling along his own path, doing exactly what he wants to do. And in doing that, he's made it to the top. The more movies he makes, the more in demand he becomes. There are more offers—more *good* offers—than he can manage, and he's been forced to become more selective.

At heart, like most people, Ewan is a mass of contradictions, the family man who loves his wife and daughter, but still enjoys going out regularly with his mates, the boy from a small Scottish town who's a star but distrustful of it all. He's human.

And he's become the most famous Scotsman since Sean Connery. For all that Sick Boy lampooned 007 in *Trainspotting*, there was a faint air of admiration about it all. Maybe, a generation from now, there'll be another film where it'll be Ewan

McGregor on the receiving end of the jokes.

For now, though, there's no stopping him. He's conquered earth, and moved to make his mark in that galaxy far, far away. It's guaranteed, though, that he'll be around for a long, long time to come, and—if he has his way—in every good film he's offered. But that's what happens when you choose to live a life that is definitely a little less ordinary.

Filmography

Television

Lipstick on Your Collar
(1993)
Giles Thomas ... Private Francis Francis
Ewan McGregor ... Private Mick Hopper
Louise Germaine ... Sylvia Berry
Kymberley Huffman ... Lisa
Peter Jeffrey ... Colonel Bernwood

WRITER: Dennis Potter
DIRECTOR: Renny Rye

Scarlet and Black
(1993)
Ewan McGregor ... Julien Sorel
Alice Krige
Stratford Johns
T. P. McKenna
Rachel Weisz

Doggin' Around
(1994)
Elliott Gould ... Joe Warren
Geraldine James ... Sarah Williams
Alun Armstrong ... Charlie Foster
Ewan McGregor ... Tom Clayton
Liz Smith ... Mrs. Thompson
Anthony Etherton ... Gary Powell

Kavanagh, QC: Nothing But the Truth
(1995)
Ewan McGregor . . . David Armstrong

Tales From the Crypt: The Cold War
(1996)
Ewan McGregor . . . Ford
Jane Horrocks . . . Girlfriend

Karaoke
(1996)
Albert Finney . . . Daniel Feeld
Julie Christie . . . Lady Ruth Balmer
Richard E. Grant . . . Nick Balmer
Alison Steadman . . . Mrs. Haynes
Hywel Bennett . . . Arthur Mallion
Ewan McGregor . . . Young Man

WRITER: Dennis Potter
DIRECTOR: Renny Rye

ER
(1997)
Ewan McGregor . . . Duncan

<u>Short Films</u>

Family Style
(1993)

Swimming With the Fishes
(1996)

<u>Film</u>

Being Human
(1993)
Robin Williams . . . Hector
John Turturro . . . Lucinnius
Anna Galiena . . . Beatrice
Vincent D'Onofrio . . . Priest
Hector Elizondo . . . Dom Paolo
Ewan McGregor . . . Alvarez

WRITER: Bill Forsyth
DIRECTOR: Bill Forsyth

Shallow Grave
(1994)
Kerry Fox . . . Juliet Miller
Christopher Eccleston . . . David Stephens
Ewan McGregor . . . Alex Law
Ken Stott . . . Detective Inspector
Keith Allen . . . Hugo
Colin McCredie . . . Cameron

WRITER: Danny Boyle
DIRECTOR: John Hodge

Bluejuice
(1995)
Sean Pertwee . . . JC
Catherine Zeta Jones . . . Chloe
Steven Mackintosh . . . Josh Tambini
Ewan McGregor . . . Dean Raymond
Peter Gunn . . . Terry Colcott
Heathcote Williams . . . Shaper

WRITER: Carl Prechezer, Peter Salmi, Tim Veglio
DIRECTOR: Carl Prechezer, Peter Salmi

Trainspotting
(1996)
Ewan McGregor . . . Mark Renton
Ewen Bremner . . . Spud
Jonny Lee Miller . . . Sick Boy
Robert Carlyle . . . Begbie
Kelly Macdonald . . . Diane

WRITER: John Hodge
DIRECTOR: Danny Boyle

Emma
(1996)
Gwyneth Paltrow . . . Emma Woodhouse
Jeremy Northam . . . Mr. Knightley
Greta Scacchi . . . Mrs. Weston
Toni Collette . . . Harriet Smith
Sophie Thompson . . . Miss Bates
Ewan McGregor . . . Frank Churchill

WRITER: Douglas McGrath
DIRECTOR: Douglas McGrath

The Pillow Book
(1996)
Vivian Wu . . . Nagiko
Yoshi Oida . . . Publisher
Ken Ogata . . . Father
Ewan McGregor . . . Jerome
Hideko Yoshida . . . Aunt/Maid
Judy Ongg . . . Mother

WRITER: Peter Greenaway
DIRECTOR: Peter Greenaway

Brassed Off
(1997)
Pete Postlethwaite . . . Danny
Tara Fitzgerald . . . Gloria Mullins
Ewan McGregor . . . Andy
Jim Carter . . . Harry
Steve Tompkinson . . . Phil
Peter Gunn . . . Simmo
Ken Colley . . . Greasley

WRITER: Mark Herman
DIRECTOR: Mark Herman

A Life Less Ordinary
(1997)
Ewan McGregor . . . Robert
Cameron Diaz . . . Celine
Holly Hunter . . . O'Reilly
Delroy Lindo . . . Jackson
Ian Holm . . . Naville
Ian McNeice . . . Mayhew

WRITER: John Hodge
DIRECTOR: Danny Boyle

Nightwatch
(1998)
Ewan McGregor . . . Martin Bells
Nick Nolte . . . Inspector Cray
Josh Brolin . . . James Coleman

Patricia Arquette . . . Katherine
Alix Koromzay . . . Joyce

WRITER: Ole Bornedal, Steven Soderburgh
DIRECTOR: Ole Bornedal

The Serpent's Kiss
(1998)
Ewan McGregor . . . Meneer Chrome
Pete Postlethwaite . . . Thomas Smithers
Greta Scacchi . . . Juliana
Richard E. Grant . . . James Fitzmaurice
Carmen Chaplin . . . Thea

WRITER: Tim Rose Price
DIRECTOR: Philippe Rousselot

Velvet Goldmine
(1998)
Ewan McGregor . . . Curt Wild
Jonathan Rhys-Meyers . . . Brian Slade
Toni Collette . . . Mandy Slade
Christian Bale . . . Arthur Stuart
Eddy Izzard . . . Jerry Divine
Emily Woof . . . Shannon

WRITER: Todd Haynes, James Lyons
DIRECTOR: Todd Haynes

Rogue Trader
(1998)
Ewan McGregor . . . Nick Leeson
Anna Friel . . . Lisa Leeson

WRITER: James Dearden
DIRECTOR: James Dearden

Star Wars: The Balance of the Force (1999)

Ewan McGregor . . . Ben Kenobi
Liam Neeson . . . Jedi Master
Natalie Portman . . . Young Queen
Ian McDiarmid . . . Senator Palpatine
Jake Lloyd . . . Anakin Skywalker

WRITER: George Lucas
DIRECTOR: George Lucas

Ewan on the Web

While it's unlikely that you'll come across Ewan himself on the Internet, since he's reportedly computer illiterate, you can still find plenty of sites dedicated to the man. These are the cream of the crop.

Dante's Ewan McGregor Homepage
(http://www.geocities.com/Hollywood/Academy/4060)
An organized little page.

Ewan McGregor Cyber Altar
(http://members.aol.com/BLUEVINYL/ secondpage.html)
Great to look at, lots of creative energy, and the animated gifs are well worth seeing.

Meghan's Home Page
(http://geocities.com/Hollywood/Studio/5252)
She's found some nice pictures, and laid out the design well.

The Unofficial Ewan McGregor Homepage
(http://www.geocities.com/~ewanmcgregor/main.html)
The king and without a doubt champion of sites. Great pictures, lots of information, frequently updated. Highly recommended.

Virtual McGregor
(http://www.enter.net/~cybernut/ewanmenu.htm)
This one offers some soundfiles and a Ewan McGregor screensaver.